History & Guide

WESTON-SUPER-MARE

Sharon Poole

History & Guide

WESTON-SUPER-MARE

Sharon Poole

TEMPUS

*This book is dedicated
to my late mother, with
love and thanks.*

First published 2002

Tempus Publishing Limited
The Mill, Brimscombe Port,
Stroud, Gloucestershire, GL5 2QG

British Library Cataloguing in Publication Data.
A catalogue record for this book is available from the British Library.

ISBN 0 7524 2631 1

Typesetting and origination by Tempus Publishing Limited
Printed in Great Britain by Midway Colour Print, Wiltshire

CONTENTS

PREFACE & ACKNOWLEDGEMENTS

In recent years, Weston-super-Mare has seen many changes and, with the start of a new millennium, it seems an appropriate time to reassess the town and its past. History has become extremely popular and many people are eager to find out more about their own locality. However, this book is not a complete history of Weston – it would take a larger volume than this to cover every event in the town's past. What I have tried to do is bring history to life through the people that made it. To this end I have allowed, where possible, the people themselves to speak. By using contemporary accounts from diaries, newspaper reports and guidebooks, I hope a feeling for time and place will become more vivid. The language used, the accounts of events and activities, residents' concerns and the aims and aspirations for the town all combine to tell the story of the development of Weston from a tiny settlement to a thriving seaside resort.

I must credit the work of previous local historians and archaeologists, in particular Chris Richards for his research on early botanists and musicians as well as his encyclopaedic knowledge of local geology, Jane Hill, archaeologist at North Somerset Museum Service, Jane Evans, Nick Corcos, Philip Beisly, Mike Tozer, Brian Brown, Vince Russett, John Loosley and John Bailey. Brian Austin is a continual source of interesting anecdotes and Ernest Baker's interviews with old residents in the 1880s has left us with invaluable memories of the early days of the resort.

The pictures are from a variety of sources including postcards and prints from private collections, as well as my own photographic archive. The original drawings and paintings are from the collections of North Somerset Museum Service and the three modern portraits are by photographer Graham Wiltshire.

CHAPTER 1
The Earliest Residents

As we look back today, it is hard to imagine how this somewhat faded English seaside resort once inspired poets and musicians, enticed the wealthiest visitors from London and other large cities, had crescents and terraces to rival nearby Bath, and led it to be nicknamed the Fair White City on the Severn Sea.

The town of Weston-super-Mare is situated in the south-west of England beside the Bristol Channel. It is protected from cold northerly winds by Weston Hill, a ridge of limestone rich in a variety of useful minerals. The limestone was laid down in the shallow tropical seas and lagoons that covered this region during the Carboniferous Period 300 million years ago. Undersea vents threw up volcanic rock that can still be seen in outcrops in the cliffs around Birnbeck Pier. The seabed, together with underlying layers of sediment, was then thrown up into mountains, which were gradually worn down into the rounded hills we see today during a period when there was a hot desert-like climate lasting millions of years. Today's settlement has developed down the southern slope of Weston Hill and spread onto the low-lying alluvial levels. At its southern edge it is protected by the rise of Bleadon Hill.

As the town was developed, builders began to find the remains of some of the earliest occupants of the area, and newspapers frequently reported

Outcrop of volcanic rock at Spring Cove.

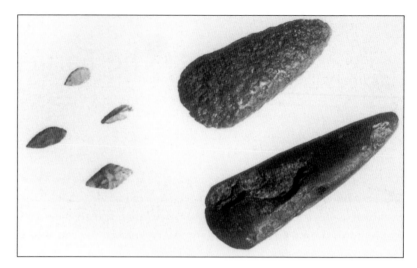

Neolithic stone axes and flint arrowheads found on Worle Hill. (Collections of North Somerset Museum Service)

discoveries such as Iron Age and Roman pottery, animal bones and human skeletons. Caves, revealed by quarrying in and around Weston, were found to contain the bones of Ice Age animals such as cave bear, reindeer, woolly mammoth, giant Irish deer and an extinct kind of rhinoceros over 120,000 years old, all of which once roamed this land.

The first people in the area were nomadic hunters, who lived for short periods in local caves while seeking food. A bone worked to a point, found in caves at Uphill, has recently been proven to be the earliest known non-stone tool made by modern humans in Britain and dates back 28,000 years. As the ice sheets melted, forests of oak, lime and other broad-leaved trees covered the countryside, providing a habitat for wild pigs, deer, wild cattle and horses, while fish and wildfowl were abundant in the wetter levels. Flint scrapers, finely-worked arrowheads and hand axes and coarse pottery are now all that remain to tell us of this time.

Gradually people stopped living a nomadic life and learned to grow crops and domesticate animals. By the Bronze Age new skills were developed and people, whilst still using stone and flint implements, learned to cast fine bronze axes and jewellery. They cremated their dead and buried the remains in funerary urns of decorated pottery, often under burial mounds or barrows. Fragments of such urns have been found in sites south of Upper Bristol Road, many of them when digging graves in Weston's Victorian cemetery.

By the time of the Iron Age, from about 650 BC, this area was extensively farmed from groups of homesteads. It was in this period that a hillfort was built on the western end of Weston Hill. This defensive stronghold, consisting of massive stone ramparts built over 2,000 years ago, has interested antiquarians from the eighteenth century onwards, although it was not until the 1850s that it was fully investigated. It was in

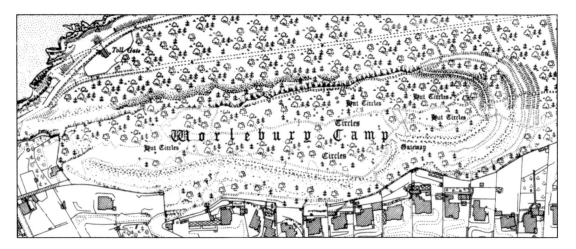

fact the first hillfort in the country to be completely excavated. There were three entrances, one at the western end, one in the southern wall and one to the north east. Evidence points to these having had timber gates set into the high stone walls. The excavations revealed many large, deep pits cut into the underlying rock, as well as hut sites and other structures. Traces of grain, including barley and wheat, and basketwork, were discovered in the pits, which were probably used for food storage throughout the winter. It is believed that people lived in farmsteads along the sides of the hill, grazing cattle and sheep on the slopes, growing wheat and other crops in small 'Celtic fields' and using the hillfort itself only as a refuge in times of trouble or for special occasions and meetings. Burials of this period were discovered at the top of Grove Park when the road was being laid in 1901. The skeletons of a family of three, a man, woman and child, were found buried in pits together with animal bones, pottery and lumps of yellow ochre. Other Iron Age burials have been discovered all around the Grove Park area, as well as near Christ Church in Montpelier and in Stafford Place.

At some point the people of Worlebury were attacked. When the survivors returned, they buried eighteen bodies in the pits among the grain and sheaves awaiting threshing, covering the bodies with stones. Here, some 1500 years later, they were discovered by the Victorian antiquarians. Most bore evidence of a violent death, the bones, both of men and women, scarred with sword cuts. Iron Age Britain was split into a variety of tribal kingdoms. Worlebury was on the southern fringes of that of the Dobunni. To the south were the Durotriges whilst over the Bristol Channel were the Silures. We may never know whether it was one of these rival tribes or invading Romans that devastated this settlement.

In the 1920s the composer Albert Ketèlbey visited the hillfort. Probably best known for such works as 'In a Monastery Garden' and 'In a

Map of Worlebury Iron Age Hillfort, from the Ordnance Survey map of 1903.

Iron Age cooking pot from Worlebury Hillfort. It is decorated in a style similar to ones found at Glastonbury Lake Village. (Collections of North Somerset Museum Service)

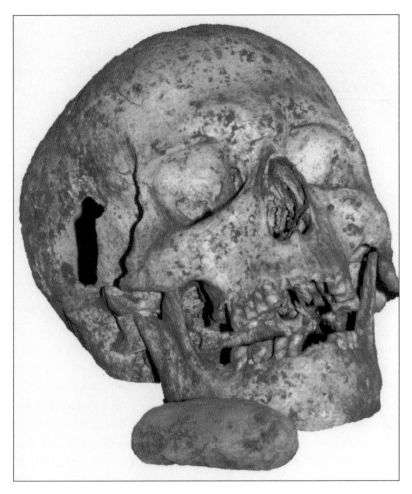

One of the skulls of the massacre victims found in the pits at Worlebury Hillfort. (Collections of North Somerset Museum Service)

Persian Market', Ketèlbey was so moved by the atmosphere of Worlebury that he wrote a musical composition:

My tone picture 'In a Camp of the Ancient Britons' was inspired by a visit to Weston-super-Mare. When I saw the gay promenade, and in the background the old ramparts, carrying the mind back to the time of Roman legions and the Druids, I felt the vividness of the contrast and I wrote music that, I hope, conveys the atmosphere of the old drama, gradually merging into present-day brightness and gaiety.

After the Romans invaded, they set about bringing southern Britain under Imperial control and Roman culture gradually became adopted by the local Britons. From finds of pottery, coins and burials, we know there were at least two sites of settlement in Roman times. The first was the area around Weston College, South Terrace and Royal Crescent where a drainage pit revealed remains of a stone building, together with large amounts of pottery of the second to fourth centuries AD, an enamelled brooch, bead, mosaic floor tiles, shells and animal bones. More recently a human burial and pottery were discovered at the rear of Royal Crescent. The second site of Roman occupation was around the area now occupied by Roslyn Avenue at Milton. The Romano-British temple on Brean Down must have been visible for miles and surely indicates a population of some size in the area, and it is even likely a smaller pagan shrine was built on Worlebury, as finds of iron nails suggest the existence of a Romano-British building of some description. Two hoards of Roman coins have also been found, eleven buried on the south-west slope of Worlebury and two hundred Late-Empire coins within the hillfort itself.

By AD 410, troubles on the eastern fringes of its empire forced Rome to withdraw from its occupation of Britain. With Imperial rule gone, the country returned to being a collection of individual kingdoms, each one frequently under threat from stronger rivals. It was now that the Saxons and North Germans began to migrate into Britain, gradually moving westwards in search of land. Christianity was introduced to the area during this period. A large Saxon settlement was established at Cheddar and their carved stonework has been discovered in churches at Rowberrow and Banwell. As with the Romans before them, Saxon culture gradually merged with that of the Britons. However, another threat soon arose – Danish raiders. By AD 870 Vikings were sailing up the Bristol Channel, launching raids inland down rivers such as the Parrett and Axe. The *Anglo-Saxon Chronicle* records that, on being driven back by the Saxons, several Danes took refuge on the islands of Flat Holm and Steep Holm from where raids were launched on the nearby coast. Holm is in fact a Danish word meaning 'river island'. In many areas, the Vikings established peaceful settlements on the mainland but nothing has yet been found to suggest this happened in North Somerset.

In fact, little has survived at all in Weston to tell us of these Dark Ages. Burials found during building works in the nineteenth century mean we can assume a small resident population. Skeletons of at least twenty people were found during the building of Park Place and Greenfield Place and when Royal Crescent was built, several small stone-walled enclosures were discovered. Each of these measured about sixteen feet long by twelve feet wide, with walls three feet high. The floors of these enclosures were paved with stones said to have been worn as if by the feet of animals. From these enclosures a paved trackway led northwards up the slope of the hill. Archaeologists believe that these were animal pens dating to the Dark Ages. Elsewhere in the town, seven skeletons were discovered at Ashcombe Park and iron coffin bands, believed to be of Saxon date, turned up in Montpelier.

The only confirmed Dark Age find is a silver ring brooch of the sixth century, found beside Monks Steps, a steep pathway linking the hamlet of Milton with Kewstoke village and its twelfth-century parish church. The network of alleys and streets around the north end of Weston High Street, close to the present church, suggest a site of Anglo-Saxon and medieval settlement, particularly when linked to the name The Worthy. This name, now surviving in Worthy Place and Worthy Lane, often indicates an Anglo-Saxon settlement and indeed, a coin of the Saxon King Edmund I was dug up here. The first church in Weston was probably established at this time, most likely as a wooden structure, replaced in the medieval period by a stone church. In the seventh and eighth centuries regional churches were founded, staffed by teams of priests who served large *parochiae*. As the Saxons gained power these areas were broken up into smaller parishes as landowners founded local churches for themselves and their tenants. Gradually a system of counties was born, each divided up into administrative districts known as 'hundreds', an area that was supposed to contain 100. Weston fell within the Hundred of Winterstoke. This ran from the boundaries of Portbury in the north to just beyond Weston-super-Mare in the south, and included a part of the Mendip Hills, taking in twenty-six parishes in total.

After the Norman invasion of 1066, land previously owned by the lords of the Saxon court was condensed into large baronies and manors and handed out to friends and supporters of William I. In 1086 the Domesday Book was compiled. Weston was not a manor in its own right at this time and fell within that of Ashcombe, now only surviving as the name of a park and in road names but once a separate village. It was then owned by the Bishop of Coutances with Herluin as tenant. Its value was listed as 100 shillings and included a hundred acres of pasture, three acres of coppice and forty acres of meadow. Other surrounding Domesday manors included Uphill, Kewstoke and Worle.

Walter of Douai held the Manor of Worle, together with many other strategic sites in Somerset. William I was fearful of an invasion being launched by the son of King Harold and set up strong defences. A wooden fortification was built at Castle Batch in the late eleventh or twelfth century. It was one of thirty-six similar fortified castles in Somerset, the next nearest being Locking Castle. However, the main village of Worle developed along the south-facing slope of the south-eastern corner of

Domesday Book entry for the Manor of Aisecome (Ashcombe).

Foxglove Cottage, then Bell House, The Scaurs, Worle, c. 1910. This medieval cruck-frame cottage is probably the oldest in Worle.

Worle Hill east of the church. At the top of the Scaurs, Foxglove Cottage is probably the oldest cottage in Worle, being of medieval cruck frame construction. Later the de Courtenay family bought this manor and it was a member of that family who, in the early years of the thirteenth century, founded Woodspring Priory. The Priory was an Augustinian monastery, built on the slopes of Middle Hope north east of Kewstoke, and founded in 1220 by William de Courtenay, a descendant of one of the murderers of Thomas à Becket.

Most of the local churches were established around the twelfth and thirteenth centuries. Worle church is of twelfth-century foundation. A few years later a tithe barn, the remaining fragments of which are now part of Hillside First School, was built beside the church. Although Worle was larger in terms of population than Weston, it is interesting that its church was valued in 1292 at eight marks, while that at Weston was valued at ten marks. A mark was worth two-thirds of a pound, making Weston £6 13s 4d and Worle £5 6s 8d. The difference in value may have been accounted for by the fact that while the economy of Worle was based on agriculture, Weston also had its fisheries. Fish were an extremely valuable commodity in medieval times and gave variety to a somewhat limited diet.

Everyday life centred around the church, and, although we do not know exactly when the one at Weston was built, we know there was a rector there in 1180, and that it had become a parish church by 1226. That was the year of the first written reference to Weston, which is in the registers of the Dean and Chapter of Wells Cathedral. The name Weston is made up of two Saxon words meaning the west *tun* or settlement. As

South front and tower of
Woodspring Priory,
c. 1906.

there were at least ten different places called Weston in Somerset,
descriptions were gradually added to tell them apart, such as North
Weston and Weston in Gordano. Our village had several different
descriptions, such as Weston Propre Worle (Weston near Worle), Weston
Juxta Mare (Weston next the sea), West Weston and, in 1314, Weston-
super-Mare (Weston on Sea). What is unusual is that we still use the

The ruins of Worle Tithe Barn, from an old print. In 1866 they were incorporated into Worle School, now Hillside First School.

Medieval Latin name today, *super* meaning on or above, and *mare* meaning sea. Most towns, such as Burnham on Sea, have anglicized their names over the centuries.

The Church held many powers. The priest of a parish was entitled to a tenth part of the main produce of the land. This was known as a tithe and was paid by all parishioners. It could include milk, wool, pigs or grain crops, which were then stored in a tithe barn. In their turn, rectors had to pay tithes to the diocese and probably got to keep little of the goods paid to them. Some demands were harder to fulfil than others. In the early thirteenth century the Rector of Weston was required to supply a tithe of 100lb of wax a year to provide candles for the High Altar at Wells Cathedral. This was a huge amount, calculated by some as amounting to the product of over one hundred hives, and it is little wonder that it was usually in arrears. Sometimes the Bishop would tour his lands, such visitations frequently causing local consternation, not least among the clergy. In 1266 the living of Weston was confiscated by the Bishop as the Rector had not bothered to attend ordinary services, although it was returned a few days later after the priest promised to be more diligent. Edward III granted the 'wreck of the sea' on Weston beach to the Bishop of Bath and Wells and in 1353, Bishop Ralph became so angry when he discovered that Weston villagers were keeping any useful beachcombings for themselves, that he called them 'sons of iniquity' and ordered a

mandate to be read in the parish church threatening offenders with excommunication and other unnamed punishments.

In 1327, fifteen landowners were paying tax on their holdings in the form of exchequer lay subsidies for the parish of Weston, with amounts varying between 6d and 5s. It is unlikely that many, if indeed any, of these people actually lived in the village, as they probably let their land to tenant farmers. Owners included Robert de Ceddar – a wealthy Bristol burgess – Roger de Hanam, Richardo le Whyte and Margeria le Grays.

When the Black Death arrived in the West County in 1348, half the population of Somerset died. Records from Woodspring Priory, which then held the right to appoint local priests, show the prior as having to appoint no less than three vicars in one month at Worle with similar situations occurring at Locking, Kewstoke and Weston. As more people died or tried to escape the plague, Bishop Ralph allowed confessions of the dying to be heard by laymen and even women.

Weston probably changed little during these years. The main street was aligned along what is now the High Street, leading southwards to the low-lying levels with their summer pastures and hay meadows, and continuing as a rough track between the marshy moor and the beach to Uphill. A medieval wayside cross stood between Weston and Uphill beside the trackway, roughly at the beach end of what is now Quantock Road. Watersill Road ran at right angles, following the line of the present Regent Street and Locking Road, petering out on the moor. At the northern end of The Street a path led up the hillside to the church and beyond to the open fields, in which the villagers grew crops, while another track followed the line of what is now Bristol Road east to the hamlets of Milton, Ashcombe and Worle. Scattered around the village were small cottages and farmhouses, built from wattle and daub with thatched roofs. On the eastern side of The Street was a stream and withy beds. Withies were young willow twigs, used in basket-making. Without the seawall, built in the nineteenth century, the beach, or strand as it was called, stretched much further inland and wind-blown sand formed dunes as far as what are now Regent and Meadow Streets. In fact the beach, which was later to become one of the town's greatest assets, could be a real problem. In winter, storms could blow enough sand to engulf a cottage, while in summer, the dunes swarmed with sand flies. As late as 1791, Collinson wrote in his *History and Antiquities of the County of Somerset*, that Weston 'lies upon the Channel northward from Uphill, on the opposite side of that rich moor, the skirts of which towards the sea are … so covered with drifts of sand'. In 1795, Richard Locke commented in his *History of Somerset* that 'Weston Supra Mare' was situated 'two miles north from Uphill from which it is separated by a large and once valuable moor which ought long since to have been inclosed and defended from

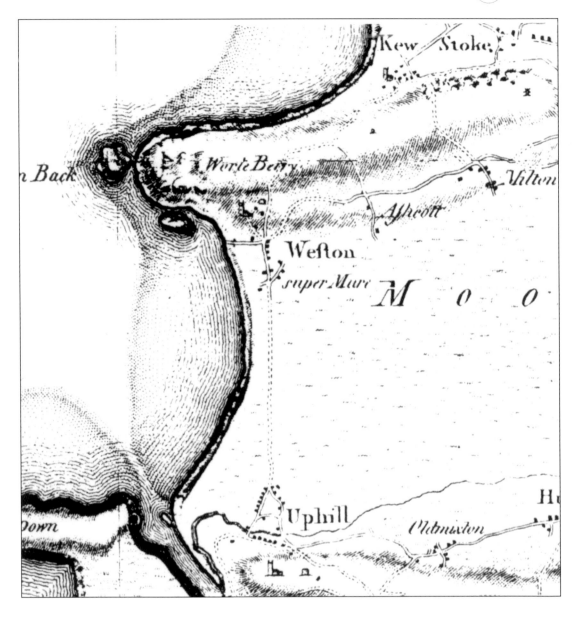

Weston-super-Mare from Day & Masters map of Somerset, 1792.

the injury it hath sustained by the sand being blown over it'.

A small creek ran inland along the line of what are now Knightstone Road and Lovers Walk towards what is now the YMCA. In 1862 an ancient boat was found while digging the foundations for Grove Villas in Bristol Road. One can imagine traders in wooden boats drawing up to the banks to exchange goods and maybe fish and other foods. The course of this creek could still be traced as late as the early nineteenth century.

Cattle and sheep were grazed on the hilltop. It had no trees at that time and would have looked much as Brean Down and Sand Point do today although a small area of ancient woodland grew at Ashcombe at the top of what is now Wood Lane. This was enclosed by a stone wall to stop sheep straying in from the hillside. There was a widespread move, after the Black Death, to turn agricultural production over to livestock more than arable. Sheep were particularly valuable, supplying milk, cheese, manure and wool. In the Middle Ages there were 47,000 sheep in Somerset and many of the county's best churches owe their beauty and rich furnishings to profits from wool.

It is easy to imagine that the villagers lived an isolated life, cut off from nearby towns and cities. However, there is no reason for the people of Weston not to have travelled. In fact they had one convenient line of communication in the sea, which afforded an easy route for fishermen to take their catch to markets south to Bridgwater or north to Bristol. Cattle would be taken to market along the drove roads to Bristol or Axbridge and even across to Wales by boat, whilst surplus produce was even taken as far as Exeter on occasion. Small villages could only support a limited number of people and men must have travelled to other villages in search of work or wives. In return, itinerant craftsmen and pedlars would have brought news of outside events to Weston.

CHAPTER 2
Early Industry and the First Visitors

The reign of Henry VIII is probably best remembered for the Dissolution of the monasteries, the Reformation and establishment of the Church of England. As the new social and religious order swept the county Henry ordered the 'obliteration and destruction of popish and superstitious books and images, so that the memory of them shall not remain in their churches and houses'. As a result, many church furnishings and decorations were destroyed or thrown away. In some cases precious relics were hidden in the hope that a time would come when they could be reinstated. It was probably at this time that a stone reliquary containing a wooden cup, said to contain the blood of the martyr Thomas à Becket, was taken from Woodspring Priory and hidden in Kewstoke church, where it remained until its discovery during building works in 1849. The Hundred of Winterstoke was sold during Henry's reign to Edward, Duke of Somerset. This was in response to the King's distrust of the Church and his wish to reduce its wealth and power.

On the military front, Henry VIII was anxious to establish an English brass industry, mainly for the manufacture of cannon. To this end he employed German prospectors to explore England and Wales for useful minerals, especially copper ore and calamine, a zinc ore, both essential to make brass. Copper ore had been mined in England and Wales since the Bronze Age but a source of calamine had not yet been discovered. On Henry's death, his successors continued the search, and were rewarded when, in 1566, Christopher Schutz and William Humfrey, Assay Master of the Mint, 'took a lease of Sir Henry Wallopp of a hill in Somersetsheere called Worley Hill and ther set Tenne or Twelve persons straungers [Germans] and Englishe on worke to moyn [mine] and search for Calamine, which the Countrymen ther do report, and gott 20 or 30 tonnes of the said stone'. It was a significant moment in the history of this area as miners moved in to extract the mineral. The calamine was sent to brass-foundries set up at Tintern in Wales and in Middlesex.

In the 1960s, one of the eighteenth-century calamine mines was broken into during quarrying at Worle, revealing the methods then used by the miners. They worked in candlelight and remains of drill holes showed that the ore was extracted using gunpowder as well as wedges, chisels and picks. It was then hauled to the surface in wooden buckets by a hand-operated windlass.

In 1736, James May of Worle was killed by a fall of rock in a calamine mine and it was shortly afterwards that mining ceased on the hill. The exact date is not known but the geologist Sir Henry de la Beche reported in 1839 that once-profitable calamine mines on Worle Hill had been for so long discontinued that he found it difficult to establish the precise nature of the occurrence of the mineral. However, other minerals, including lead, continued to be mined in other parts of Weston well into the nineteenth century.

During the Tudor period, England was threatened in turn by both France and Spain, not to mention civil uprisings, and the Government's finances were stretched to the limit. Every large landowner in the country was required to contribute cash, or be labelled a 'recusant'. In 1586 the Rector of Weston contributed £3 2s 6d towards preparations, and Edward Arthur, the Lord of the Manor of Ashcombe, received a request for a loan of £20 for 'the view, training and sorting of weapons and for training horse soldiers.' Similar requests went out to Edward Carre of Worle, Christopher Payne of Hutton and other landowners in the locality. There was no regular standing army at this time and musters were taken regularly in every village and town, listing the numbers of able men ready to serve and what arms they could supply and use. A manuscript in the British Museum showing the 'Coast of England upon Severn', and attributed to the reign of Henry VIII, depicts a series of fortifications down the coast including one at Weston, but no evidence has been found that it was ever built.

By 1470, Ashcombe Manor had been divided into two – Ashcombe and West Weston, although they remained closely linked in ownership. In 1572 Edward Baesh of Stanstede in Hertfordshire was owner. A deed of that date grants a twenty-one-year lease to Hugh Smyth of Long Ashton and Matthew Smyth of London to 'All that parcel of ground or little yland commonly called Ankers Head ... and all the proffittees and prehemynence of the fowle and fishings in or upon the said parcel of ground.' In addition, the Smyths were allowed to choose a piece of ground on the common or wasteland on which to build a small cottage for a gamekeeper, the whole deal costing them 4d a year. The area called Ankers Head in the deed referred to what we know today as Birnbeck and was the site of Weston's main fishery. However, the document made it very clear that the Smyths were not allowed any of the catch from the fishing stalls that were leased to the manorial tenants.

Later the Arthur family of Clapton owned the manors until in 1636 they passed by marriage to the Winter family. In 1695 the estates were sold to Colonel John Pigott under a double transfer and the two manors

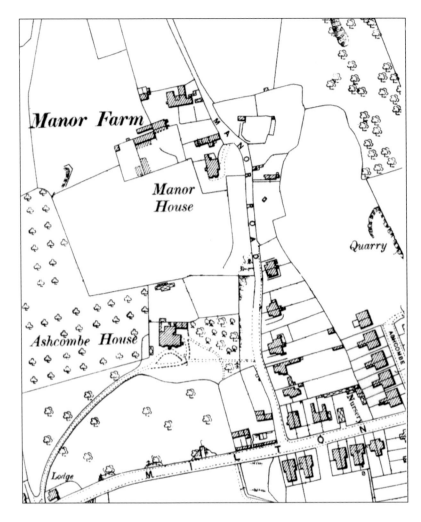

The remains of Ashcombe Manor as recorded on the Ordnance Survey map of 1902. Manor Farm, Manor House and Ashcombe House have all since been demolished, although the lodge survives next to the southern entrance to Weston Cemetery.

were again incorporated as one. John Pigott also owned the manor of Brockley, which he had inherited from his father, the Rt Hon. Colonel Thomas Pigott. Thomas had married a rich widow, Florence Smyth, daughter of the first Baron Poulet who owned land in Clevedon, Kenn and Yatton. After the Restoration of the monarchy in 1660, Thomas asked Florence to live in Ireland where he owned estates. She refused, wishing to remain close to her only son, Hugh Smyth of Ashton Court, so her husband purchased the manor of Brockley, which included Brockley Court, where Florence chose to live. When John Pigott became lord of the manor, he expanded the family's land holdings by purchasing not only the manors of Weston-super-Mare and Ashcombe but also land at Woodspring Priory. Two years later, John built a small holiday cottage in The Grove at Weston. This copse, now Grove Park, was situated on the eastern side of the rectory, and close to the parish

'Mr Pigott's Cottage by the Bristol Channel'. This eighteenth-century wash drawing is the earliest yet found of Weston-super-Mare. It shows what would become Grove House, together with a small thatched cottage since demolished, to its right. (Collections of North Somerset Museum Service)

Fragment of a wine bottle, found in Grove Park with a seal for I.(J.)P., 1717. This was probably the property of John Pigott. (Collections of North Somerset Museum Service)

church. In the collections of North Somerset Museum Service is a wash drawing of 'Mr Pigott's Cottage near the Bristol Channel' dated about 1780. It is the earliest illustration so far found of Weston.

A new rectory was also built sometime in the seventeenth century, probably to replace a medieval structure. Known as Glebe House, it is the oldest building surviving in Weston today. In 1642, during the English Civil War, the rector, Christopher Sadbury, sided with the Royalists. This offended the local villagers who had Parliamentarian sympathies. This situation came to a head in 1644 when the rector sent intelligence to the local Royalist commander, enabling the soldiers to capture some rebel villagers who were then temporarily imprisoned in the Rectory. The following year Sir Thomas Austen and his troops came to plunder the village. However, the rebels joined with those at Milton and Worle and routed the soldiers. Later, when the troops rallied, Sadbury betrayed the names of all the villagers who had opposed him. When the war ended with the King's defeat and execution, a charge of High Delinquency was brought against Sadbury. The court ordered that his estates be seized in recompense. However, the order was never enforced and he escaped unpunished. The rectory has been enlarged and altered over the years but many original seventeenth-century interior features can still be traced.

During this period the villagers of Weston, then thirty-five families, continued to live by fishing, farming, teasel growing and collecting seaweed. Seaweed was a useful fertilizer for crops and was later carted or sailed up to Bristol to provide potash for the glassworks. Teasels were used in the woollen industry to give a fine nap to the cloth and were exported to the Gloucestershire mills and even, it is thought, as far as Yorkshire. Besides meat and fish, vegetables were grown in small plots and other foods were provided by the landscape. Blackberries grew in the hedgerows. Watercress was gathered from the stream beside the main street and samphire was collected from the rocks around Birnbeck Island.

In the seventeenth century a windmill appears to have been built on the hilltop, just above the Town Quarry. It became derelict by the 1770s, probably being superseded by Worle Hill mill. This was built in 1765, replacing an older one which burnt down. It is unlikely there was enough grain to keep two mills in production. The next nearest mill would have been at Uphill, although this too was derelict by 1792. This follows a general pattern in Somerset as changes in land use caused many mills to be run down.

Weston is renowned for its mild climate but this is not always the case. In 1606 there were severe floods when the sea defences collapsed. The water in Kingston Seymour church rose to five feet and a large number of people drowned, including eleven at Uphill. Weston, Worle and Kewstoke all suffered too but the exact details went unrecorded. In 1683 a Great Frost hit the Mendips. Deep snow lay from Christmas to March and both cattle and people lost their lives. In 1815 there was another severe frost lasting sixteen weeks. Samuel Norvill recalled that he had to

Pencil drawing of Worle, 1826. St Martin's church and the cottages at the top of The Scaurs can be seen in the centre, whilst Worle Hill windmill overlooks the village. (Collections of North Somerset Museum Service)

walk to Worle on the frozen snow which was on a level with the tops of the hedges, in order to fetch bread as there was none left in Weston. Floods and gales again hit the area in the early eighteenth century, destroying crops, homes and trees; a phenomenon that continues to the present day, with notable gales in 1903 and 1981 causing similar structural damage.

Now the first stirrings of a new industry began, one that would change Weston's fortunes forever. Up to the seventeenth century, inland spas were the holiday resorts for the rich, and invalids went to places such as Harrogate, Bath and Leamington to drink the natural mineral springs, and sometimes bathe in the waters. Richard Nash became Master of Ceremonies in Bath in 1705 and changed it from a disorderly town full of gamblers, into the most fashionable place in Britain. Elegant Assembly Rooms, pump-rooms, circulating libraries and theatres were built and were soon copied in other spa towns.

Despite these pleasant distractions, the medicinal side was taken very seriously. Those people that could afford it were as obsessed with their health as we are today, and spas offered hope to invalids at a time when medical treatment was basic and painful. However, exaggerated claims were often made for the healing powers of the waters and it was this propaganda that brought the first glimmers of interest in sea water.

In the seventeenth century some doctors began to 'discover' curative powers in cold-water bathing. Dr Whittie of Scarborough claimed that the sea could cure gout while Sir John Floyer, a doctor at Buxton, recommended cold baths for vigour, strength and hardiness and considered hot springs, such as at Bath, 'corrupted manners and made bodies effeminate'.

Slowly, resorts developed, usually at places close to large inland towns, as travelling any distance was difficult. Bathing brought a few visitors to towns such as Eastbourne, Deal and Brighthelmstone, a small fishing port an easy distance from London. It was another doctor, Richard Russell, who transformed Brighthelmstone into what we know today as Brighton. In 1750 he published his *Dissertations on the use of Seawater in Diseases of the Glands*. Inland spas were still popular, but many real invalids must have begun to realize that they had little to offer. In addition the fashionable pleasure seekers had begun to look for new distractions as the spas became too popular. Russell's book became an immediate best-seller and other doctors began to send their patients to the seaside.

Just one more thing was required to make the coast acceptable in society – royal approval. The Prince Regent paid a short visit to Brighton in 1783, and enjoyed it so much he returned the following year with a large retinue. In 1789 George III was prescribed a course of sea bathing and headed for Weymouth, where female bathing attendants helped him into the water from his bathing machine as a band, concealed in another bathing machine, played the national anthem. A bathing machine was a wooden hut on wheels with a door at each end. The bather entered the machine at the top of the beach and changed into bathing dress while the machine was wheeled, by horse or man, down to the water's edge. There, the bather could descend straight into the water unseen from the promenade. King George enjoyed Weymouth so much, he paid annual visits thereafter and the seaside became the place to be.

Other factors also played their part in making the coast fashionable. By the mid-seventeenth century a new interest in science led people to search out and catalogue plants, flowers and animal species and to explore the geology of their country. In fact, Weston came to be known in the wider world for its botany long before any other of its attractions. In the late eighteenth century the Napoleonic Wars began. Since people could no longer take the Grand Tour of Europe, they began to explore Britain instead, a move fuelled by the Romantic movement in literature and art, which also aroused an interest in the unspoilt beauty of the English countryside.

And so the tiny village of Weston-super-Mare, close to the cities of Bristol and Bath, began to see strangers in its midst – not country men looking for work, but scientists with collecting jars and notebooks, and wealthy tourists with sketchbooks, drawing instruments and paints.

The earliest record of a visit to Weston-super-Mare is that of a herbalist, John Parkinson. Parkinson was an apothecary and herbalist to King Charles II and recorded that he had seen the fern wall rue 'on the Rockes near Weston-super-Mare'. At the end of the seventeenth century, another visitor was Leonard Plukenet, a physician and superintendent of the Royal Gardens at Hampton Court. He collected many plants from the village, including sea spleenwort, a maritime fern. In the eighteenth century 'plant hunting' became a popular hobby among the rich, who competed with each other to have the rarest and most interesting plants in their gardens and conservatories. In 1726, the German botanist, Jacob Dillenius, the first Professor of Botany at Oxford University, toured Somerset with Samuel Brewer, who later became head gardener to the Duke of Beaufort. Among their discoveries here were sea campion on the slopes above Knightstone, and a previously unrecorded species of grass on the down at Uphill and Brean. Unique to this area, this grass later became known as Somerset hair-grass.

Botany was not the only scientific interest bringing visitors. In 1758 the Reverend Catcott was touring Mendip studying the geology. As he rode along Worle Hill and down into Weston village, he noted many small clams on the beach and the sand dunes 'in some places raised to Banks three or four feet high'.

Wall rue. This fern is a common sight in many of the limestone walls of the town.

Another attraction was the number of 'miraculous wells' in the village. In 1791 Collinson wrote of 'a remarkable well, which at ebb tide is full, but sinks as the tide comes in, and becomes quite empty at high water.' One of these wells was at Grove House, while another was reported at the bottom of Highbury Road in the grounds of Devonshire Cottage (now part of the Bayside Hotel). Weston also boasted chalybeate springs, rich in iron, whilst the Dripping Well Cave at Spring Cove was the site of a freshwater spring where water trickled out through the rocks and into a natural 'font'. Of all of the above, only the Dripping Well can still be seen, although the cave that originally sheltered it collapsed in a landslide in the nineteenth century.

In 1773 Dr Langhorne, rector of Blagdon and the translator of Plutarch, visited Weston-super-Mare. Here he met the philanthropist and social reformer Hannah More, who was convalescing at Uphill. The

Lieutenant William Leeves.

growing popularity of Weston, and possibly his friendship with Hannah More, encouraged the Revd William Leeves of Wrington to build a seaside holiday cottage on the dunes. William began his career in the army, achieving the rank of lieutenant, before deciding to resign his commission and take holy orders. He became Rector of Wrington at the age of thirty. Leeves was a talented musician and composed the popular tune to the ballad *Auld Robin Gray*. Whilst in Weston he would join in musical evenings with his close neighbours, the Pigotts, at Grove House. When not in residence himself, he rented the cottage out to friends. A later description of Leeves' Cottage describes it as a 'quaint and curious structure, with a high thatched roof, and square-headed windows, shaded by the tea plant, which profusely covers the walls of the house. On the ground floor are two little odd-looking gabled projections, like porches, one of which has a window inserted in its front, and attached to the dwelling is a stable, and coach-house or barn with high folding doors – a lawn, diversified with shrubs, and a few flower beds, ornament the enclosed ground before the house, separated from the road by a wall about three feet in height'. Reverend Leeves died in 1828 and the cottage was sold to a retired East India merchant, Mr Clemons, who, it was remembered by a visitor in 1829, kept a golden eagle on display in the front garden, chained by the leg to a large tree.

Print of Leeves' Cottage. Only the right-hand part remains today.

Six years after Leeves' Cottage was completed, the first advertisement for holiday accommodation in the area was placed in the *Bristol Journal*. This read:

> For health and Sea Bathing. At Uphill Jane Biss and Son most respectfully inform the public that they have fitted up two commodious houses for the reception of families or single persons during the summer at reasonable terms.

Soon afterwards, William Sheppard of the Ship Inn at Uphill was advertising an 'elegant bathing machine' available 'For Company, during the Season'. Uphill was clearly trying to cash in on the bathing boom and in 1826 a Sea Bathing Infirmary was opened there for 'affording relief to diseased objects of charity'! Funded by charitable donations, it closed a couple of years later due to lack of patients. Not long afterwards, Uphill's popularity petered out in favour of Weston with its sweeping sands and easier access.

The early visitors found a primitive but charming village. A local historian, Ernest Baker, interviewed some of the oldest inhabitants in the 1880s. Samuel Norvill was born in Weston in 1800 and remembered the village when there was no hotel, no public house and no shop. He recalled:

> There was no High Street: it was called The Street, and very narrow it was too, there was only just room for one putt or cart to pass down it at a time. On the East side there was ditch, and on the West a hedge banked up with stones to keep the earth back. The street itself was always very muddy and dirty; some stones were thrown down loosely on one side to make a sort of footpath... Midway there was a withy bed, in which refuse fish were generally thrown... Nearly everybody kept geese, they paid so well; you see, they could run about over the common all day, and so didn't cost much to keep. The feathers were plucked off the live birds once a year and taken to Bristol and other towns to sell.

Plans were already afoot, however, to turn this rustic idyll into the busy seaside resort we know today.

CHAPTER 3
The Village Awakes

The lord of the manor from 1794 was John Pigott, the great great nephew of Colonel John. He was a man of wide-ranging interests and never married. He spent much of his time in France, where he visited Voltaire and frequently left his younger brother, Wadham, to manage the estates. In 1816 John died in Calais on his way home from France and his brother became lord of the manor in his own right. In common with many second sons of the landed gentry, Wadham had entered the church and became acting Rector of Weston. As this gave him two residences in close proximity – Glebe House and Grove House – he chose to live in Grove House and let the Rectory. Also unmarried, Wadham was the first of the Pigotts to make his permanent home at Weston, rather than at Brockley. George Bennett, a solicitor and antiquarian of Banwell, arrived in the autumn of 1804 and commented that:

> This village is much frequented of late in the Summer and Autumn for the benefit of sea air and bathing, several good lodging-houses been having been lately erected for the reception of company… The Rev. Wadham Pigott, an elegant and popular preacher, is the present curate of the parish, and he has a neat and comfortable house, at which he generally resides the whole year.

Meanwhile, Weston's potential had been spotted and small but significant changes began to take place. In 1807 two local men, Richard Parsley and John Cox, persuaded John Pigott to sell some of his land holdings to them, including the old 'auster tenements'. These were fishermen's huts with small parcels of land attached. Cox and Parsley then applied for an Enclosure Award. As with all such Acts, it enabled roads to be formally mapped out and tenants, owners and land use established. Two quarries – the Town Quarry in South Road and another in Manor Road – were designated for common use for building stone and road gravel. Fences replaced the old leap-gate to keep animals from straying from the Hill and hedges of sedge were planted in the dunes in an effort to keep the sand from blowing inland and contaminating pasture. The result was that land holdings were consolidated, placing owners in a good position to then build on the land or sell off lots to speculators – which is

SOMERSETSHIRE.

Weston-super-Mare Inclosure.

Notice is hereby given,

That the COMMISSIONERS appointed for carrying into Effect the
Act of Parliament for this Inclosure, will proceed to

Sell (in Fee) by Auction,

At the House of Joseph Leman, known by the Sign of the NEW INN,

Situate in the Parish of WORLE, in the County of Somerset,

On Monday, the 8th Day of July, 1811,

Between the Hours of FOUR and SIX in the Afternoon,

THE UNDER-MENTIONED

LANDS,

Subject to such Conditions as shall be then produced.

Lot 1.—A Piece of LAND, Part of Weston-super-Mare Moor, containing by Admeasurement
one Acre and an Half, (near the House of the Rev. Mr. Lewis,) bounded Northward by an intended Road, Southward by Lot 3, Eastward by Lot 2, and Westward by the Sea Beach.

Lot 2.—A Piece of LAND, Part of the said Moor, containing by Admeasurement One Acre
and an Half, bounded Northward by the said intended Road, Southward by Lot 3, Eastward by
Part of the said Moor, and Westward by Lot 1.

Lot 3.—A Piece of LAND, Part of the said Moor, containing by Admeasurement Two Acres,
Three Roods, and Ten Perches, bounded Northward by Lots 1 and 2, Southward by Lot 4, Eastward by the said Moor, and Westward by the Sea Beach.

Lot 4.—A Piece of LAND, Part of the said Moor, containing by Admeasurement Five Acres,
bounded Northward by Lot 3, Southward and Eastward by the said Moor, and Westward by the
Sea Beach.

These Lands are put in small Lots, and selected for Sale for the Accommodation of Persons
inclined to build Houses near the Sea and the Village of Weston-super-Mare.

For viewing the Premises, apply to Mr. RICHARD PARSLEY, of Weston-super-Mare, and
for further Particulars and Conditions of Sale, to Mr. JAMES STAPLES, Land-Surveyor, at
his Office, No. 7, Queen-square, Bristol, or to Messrs. SAMUEL and JOHN BAKER,
Solicitors, Blagdon, near Bristol.

RICHARD BISHOP, *Auctioneer.*

By Order of the said Commissioners,

S. BAKER, Clerk.

BROWN, Printer, Mirror Office, Small-Street, Bristol.

*Poster advertising plots
of land for sale in 1811
as a result of the
Enclosure Act.*

exactly what Parsley and Cox set about doing. The Weston Act was
passed in 1810, with the Award map being completed in 1815.

Parsley, a farmer and captain in the West Mendip Militia, later built
himself a smart house on the then outskirts of the village with the profits
from his speculations. Built in 1828, it was named Whitecross House
after the medieval stone wayside cross on the beach near Uphill, the
remains of which Parsley removed and built into his new home. Later,

after a disagreement between himself and Bishop Henry Law, Parsley erected a 40ft-high conical tower topped by a bishop's mitre, in one of his fields. As an insult to the bishop the base of the tower was used as a pig sty. After a reconciliation, the mitre was removed and the tower rededicated to the Reform Bill. It stood until about 1890 on a site now occupied by Nos 2 and 3 Ellenborough Park Road. His house can still be seen, behind the Victoria Methodist church in Station Road, where it is used as their parish room.

Despite its growing size, the village still had no shop or inn, although most farmers would have made their own cider. Bread could be baked at home and chickens, pigs and geese kept for eggs and meat, but other provisions had to be bought in Worle, Banwell or from itinerant traders, and it was not uncommon for a couple of strong men to walk to Worle Brewery and return with a barrel of beer carried from a pole on their shoulders. When the bread cart came round, Hannah Gould used to buy

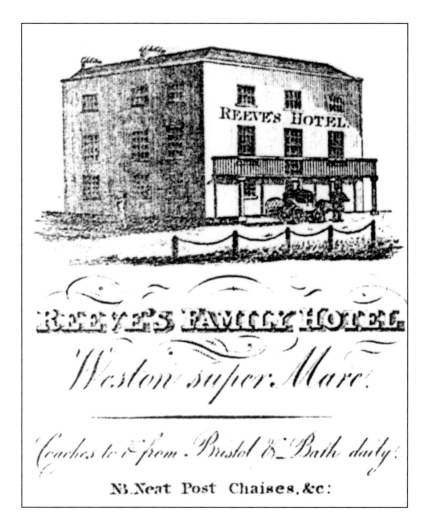

Newspaper advertisement for The Hotel, then owned by Mr Reeves, 1838.

up a quantity of loaves and retail them, displaying them on a table with a cloth over them. One visitor, here for her health in 1802, was dismayed to find such primitive conditions: 'They were so badly off for provisions that frequently they were obliged to eat bread which was completely turned mouldy and their substitute for butter was generally liquefied bacon fat.'!

It was clear by now that to continue to attract a rising number of visitors, a hotel was required. Till now the choice was between lodging with a local family or renting a house, neither option providing much in the way of comfort or facilities. Parsley and Cox, together with two other landowners, James Capell and Richard Fry, invested in the project together. The site chosen was originally occupied by an old farmhouse with barns and outbuildings, all of which burnt down on Whit Sunday 1792. Close to the beach and opposite Leeves' Cottage, The Hotel was designed with the main public rooms facing south. Later stables and lock-up coach-houses for the carriages of visitors were built at the rear. To provide milk, The Hotel had its own cows, which grazed in the Hotel Field, now the site of the Winter Gardens, and two bathing machines were available on the beach for the use of guests.

The foundation stone was laid in 1807, accompanied by a ceremony at which all the villagers watched whilst the West Mendip Militia fired volleys in all directions. However, the venture was fraught with difficulties from the start. In June 1808 Wadham Pigott wrote to his friend, the Bristol artist George Cumberland, that 'The cold weather has kept back the company from this place; now they begin to swarm a little. The Hotel is unfinished and I have my doubts of its ever answering as such'. The Hotel finally opened in July 1810 but trade fluctuated and it was not open regularly until 1814 when greater numbers of visitors made it financially viable. Over the years the Royal Hotel, as it is currently called, has been enlarged and altered but it is still accepting guests after some 200 years.

George Cumberland stayed in Weston on and off between 1802 and 1805, in the hope that bathing in sea-water would cure his chronic gout. He rented the Rectory from Wadham Pigott and has left a wealth of correspondence which provides a fascinating insight into life in Weston at that time. He spent many hours at musical evenings with his neighbours, the Reverends Wadham Pigott and William Leeves. A letter of 1805 from Cumberland's daughter Lavinia, then staying in the village, to her father back in Bristol, gives a glimpse of the increased demand for lodgings:

> Mamma, Georgiana and myself walked to Worle this morning on purpose to see if we could engage Henville's cart but could not. We

thought it necessary to let you know that we can get no conveyance here, that you might try to get a cart to be here so that we might get away Tuesday week as Mrs Sheppard has let her house and the people are to come in Wednesday week. I hope you understood that we must quit this place on Tuesday week as there are no other lodgings to be had.

The Royal Hotel as it is today. The oldest part, dating to 1807, is centre right of this photograph.

The cottages of the locals were usually built facing north or south, that is side on to the prevailing westerly winds. These natives knew all about the fierce gales of autumn and winter, which blew sand up to the levels of their roofs and flooded the low-lying fields. As the newcomers built their smart summer residences, they had other ideas and built them to face the sea. They wanted to make the most of the stunning views, renowned sunsets and bracing air. Belvedere was the first private mansion built. It was constructed in 1811 for Isaac Jacobs who ran the Non-such glassworks in Redcliffe, Bristol. George Cumberland painted several watercolours of the Bristol glassworks and it is possible that it was he who introduced Jacobs to the delights of Weston. Alternatively, seaweed was regularly carted up to the glassworks to be burnt to provide potash and he may have known of the village for that reason. In any event, his villa was situated on a prime site, which, before the building of the early promenade, was virtually on the strand itself. Today part of Carlton Mansions occupies the site. When the Reverend John Skinner, vicar of Camerton, came to visit Weston in November 1819 he wrote in his diary:

Weston seems to be rapidly increasing and, as long as the whim lasts it may answer to engage in the speculation of builders and

Bristol doctors, but I think that the obstacles are so great to its becoming a permanent place that no one risqué too much money in erecting houses for the Company, although Mr Jacobs, I find, spent upwards of £5000 in his Marine Villa built on the sand facing the muddy estuary from whence he may contemplate its chestnut-coloured waves, once at least in the day at high water, and the remainder enjoy a wide expanse of dark slime.

The notoriety of Weston mud clearly goes back a long way! Isaac Jacobs enjoyed his house for just six or seven years as money difficulties forced its sale. Belvedere was put up for auction in 1819, a year before Jacobs was declared bankrupt. It was then divided into two houses, but it is clear that it had been a very substantial property since, even when converted into two, each consisted of a basement with lobby, servants hall, cellars, butler's and china pantries, scullery and larder. On the first floor, the main door was reached by an 'elevated entrance from a handsome terrace'. There was a drawing room, dining room, billiard room and two best bedrooms. On the next floor were five more bedrooms and bathrooms. The sale advertisement ended by saying that 'The whole forming, if thrown into one house, a most desirable Marine Residence for any nobleman or Gentleman of fortune'.

A variety of choice building plots regularly came up for sale now, and it was not long before Weston had a number of bright new houses with sea views available for rent. A house could command up to six guineas a week, a considerable fortune for a villager used to surviving on what he could grow or catch. The cost did not deter visitors as the papers reported that 'Weston-super-Mare has this season overflowed with fashionables and invalids – not a lodging or house is unoccupied'. The resident population was now 163.

In 1815 an anonymous writer in the *Bristol Mirror* said that he was 'somewhat surprised that Weston-super-Mare, a village so beautifully situated for the salubrity of its air, and containing so many local advantages should not have obtained more general recommendation... The lodging houses in this place are many, and though some of them are not of the first description of fashionable elegance, yet a considerable portion of comfort may be obtained in most of them...'. That same year a visitor, known to us today only as TGR, painted a charming set of five watercolours which together show a panoramic view of the whole village. Paintings are our only record of how places looked in these days before photography and this set depict a place in transition. To the north is the old parish church, surrounded by thatched cottages and farmsteads with the three-story Hotel in the centre. In the second painting, thatched cottages of old Weston are interspersed with new taller properties with

Claremont House with its bath house, from a print of c. 1850. Billy Board's cottage can be seen in the centre.

tiled roofs. As the artist's viewpoint moves round one can see the new lodging houses in Wellington Lane and a bathing machine on the sands. On the seafront, there was no building north of Leeves' Cottage, save for Billy Board's tiny lodge at the entrance to the West Field. This was all about to change.

In January 1817 Claremont Lodge, a lodging house with private bath house, was built at Anchor Head, where the centre of Claremont Crescent is today. The Reverend Skinner visited Weston in June 1818 and called Anchor Head the 'new bathing place' while John Rutter added that 'It is inaccessible to machines, but is romantic, secluded, and convenient at all tides, so that ladies frequently resort to it for bathing.' Bathing had a set ritual since one did not bathe for enjoyment, but for its health-giving effects. Most resorts had a bathing woman, to assist nervous bathers and to forcibly duck the reluctant invalid or screaming child under the water. At Weston it fell to Jane Gill and Betty Muggleworth. At Anchor Head an old sail was spread between the rocks to shelter the ladies as they changed into coarse linen shifts before walking down the pebbly beach to the water. In August 1817 Mrs Rose Roberts wrote to her husband in Bristol, 'I drink the salt water in the morning, but do not bathe, being fearful of venturing my delicate frame out amongst the waves. I do not think I shall bathe. The gowns they make use of are such nasty looking things I do not think I could put one of them on'. Bathing was strictly segregated and men's and ladies' areas kept well apart. In August 1811, Hugh Hodges was fined £1 and forced to make a public apology when he was caught naked on the most public part of the sands one Saturday. Spotted by the magistrate out with his daughter, he was told the fine would have been greater had not the daughter been short-sighted!

The locals still relied on agriculture and fishing for their living, but the potential in the new tourism was not lost on them! It was not unknown for some fishermen to take tourists out to Steep Holm or other islands for 6d a head, and then, after landing them, to charge an extra 3d to return them to Weston! The local fishing boat was the flatner. These were built both at Weston and Bridgwater, and were designed with flat bottoms and shallow draughts so they could be sailed in very little water and beached upright. The main fish catches were sprats, dabs, cod, skate, shrimp and the occasional salmon. The first salmon caught each season had to be taken to the lord of the manor at Brockley. Samuel Norvill recalled, 'I carried up the largest one ever caught here. It weighed thirty-two pounds and a quarter and I rode up to Brockley on a pony with it. I caught it on the west side of Knightstone in a net on the mud…. Whoever took the fish to Brockley was given half-a-crown and as much as he and his pony could eat and drink'. Some fishing took place off Knightstone, but the main fisheries were at Birnbeck Island. 'Stalls' of stow nets were used, consisting of nets hanging from vertical stakes driven into the mud. The fish were caught in the nets as the tide ebbed. The problem with this method was that, in the period between the tide turning and the fishermen collecting the catch, the fish were exposed to hungry seagulls. For this reason, 'gull-yellers' were employed. These men lived in a hut on Birnbeck Island during the summer months, frightening the gulls away

Pencil drawing of Birnbeck Island, 1826. This shows the fishing stalls and nets, as well as the gull-yeller's hut. (Collections of North Somerset Museum Service)

from the fish by shouting and throwing stones. It is said that Bill Hurle of Ashcombe could be heard as far away as Congresbury! The fisheries were owned by the manor and leased to the fishermen, sometimes for a number of years, sometimes for life.

It was at Birnbeck that a tragic accident occurred in 1819. Whilst the Elton family of Clevedon Court were staying in Weston they went to visit Birnbeck. The two eldest sons began to hunt for crabs and shells on the natural rocky causeway that connected the island with the mainland at low tide. They became so absorbed that they failed to notice the rising tide and became cut off. Alerted to the danger they tried to reach the shore but the youngest, aged thirteen, was soon out of his depth and was swept away by the fierce currents. The elder boy tried to rescue him but both were lost. As soon as the water was deep enough a boat was launched by Colonel Rogers and a search began but neither was found. Their bodies were later recovered, one at Newport in Wales, the other washed up at Clevedon. A sad postscript to the story was that Colonel Rogers himself later caught pneumonia as a result of his fruitless search and he too died. There is a marble memorial to him in the chancel of the parish church. Even today many holidaymakers underestimate the treacherous mud and tidal currents despite the warning signs, and frequently require the assistance of the lifeboat or coastguard.

Another local landmark tells us of the significance of the fish catch. Visitors, walking the hill will have come across a pile of stones or cairn just before the fork to the Hillfort. Known as Peakwinnard or Picwinna, it was believed to bring good luck to fishermen. We will probably never know the exact meaning of the name but many believe that it refers to Wina, a seventh-century bishop of Wessex. Fishermen would pass the spot on their way to the Birnbeck fishery and cast a stone on the heap

Peak Wina (Picwinna) Cairn in Weston Woods, c. 1910.

while reciting the following verse, 'Picwinna, Picwinna, Pick me a good dish of fish, For my dinner.' During the nineteenth century the cairn attracted the attention of several antiquarians, including Charles Dymond who investigated Worlebury Hillfort. Dymond excavated the cairn thinking it might have had its origins as a prehistoric burial mound but found nothing to substantiate this idea.

Smuggling was rife on this part of the coast. From the early sixteenth century the Customs limit of the port of Bristol stretched down as far as Uphill. Woodspring Bay was a favourite spot to bring goods ashore, as it was sheltered, sandy and well away from the nearest Revenue Officer who was stationed at Uphill. It was here in 1783 that ten barrels of brandy were confiscated from their hiding place in the woods. Other records tell of a long-running battle of wills between the smugglers and the authorities. In 1801 a Weston fishing boat was caught with brandy and tobacco hidden under the fish. Two years later, four villagers were tried for stealing part of the cargo of rum from the *Rebecca*. The ship was wrecked off Cardiff on its journey from Jamaica to Bristol and part of the cargo conveniently washed up on local beaches, only to be carted off by delighted locals, including farmers who filled their milk pails with the liquor. The four men were acquitted, but the case served as a warning to others. In some ways the fight against smuggling does not appear to have been taken very seriously since the local coastguards consisted of a one-eyed man, another with one leg and an eighty-year-old! Smuggling was not just the pastime of fishermen. Even the squire was involved. Another local character of the time was Patty Parsons, supposedly the local witch or wise-woman. She lived in a small cottage in Kewstoke with a tree growing through it and out of the roof. Oddly, she was very friendly with the squire, even dining with him on occasion, and modern research by Brian Austin suggests that she may have been part of a smuggling ring, letting it be known that she would be out and about on a certain night, so keeping the locals indoors with their windows shut and doors bolted and giving smugglers a free rein for their activities. We will never be sure, but the fear of witchcraft still had the power to frighten people in those days when some would swear that Patty could turn people into rabbits! Indeed, when renovations took place on the old Bath House at Knightstone in 1998, a child's shoe was discovered under floorboards. This was a common folk remedy believed to ward off evil spirits!

By the early years of the nineteenth century, Weston featured regularly in the Bristol newspapers, then the nearest town with a regular press. They give an impression of a growing town, with plenty of advertisements for building plots or new property and special events being organized, such as regattas and balls. The lists of arrivals published in the papers from 1813 onwards give some idea as the wealth and class of visitors – Baroness

D'Escury, Colonel, Mrs and Miss Rogers, General and Mrs Moore, Lady Lilford and family, Sir E. Hartopp and, in August 1819, Mrs Thrale, the friend of Dr Johnson, to whom he wrote his *Letters from the Hebrides*. A letter she wrote to Sir James Fellowes of Bognor Rocks, Sussex, paints a vivid picture of Weston:

> This little place is neither gay nor fashionable, yet full as an Egg.... No market ... but I don't care about that... The breezes here are most salubrious; no land nearer than North America, when we look down the Channel... Who would be living at Bath now? The Bottom of the town a Stewpot, the top a Gridiron, and London in a State of Defence or Preparation for Attack or some strange Situation, while poor little Weston is free from Alarms.... We have swarms of Babies here, and some bathe good humouredly enough while others scream and shriek as if they were going to Execution.

In 1819, following the end of the Peninsular War and a number of poor harvests, the country went into a depression. There were many local farm auctions as people quit the land. Tourism however, continued to grow, giving hope and opportunity to those willing to embrace it.

CHAPTER 4
Village to Resort

Howe's baths opened on Knightstone Island in July 1820. Mr Howe was a parasol maker of Bristol. Together with his partner, Charles Taylor, a carpenter at Yatton, they set about taming this inhospitable rocky island and providing Weston's first medicinal spa. During excavations for the baths, a huge human skeleton, together with another cremation in a pottery urn, were found. The male, probably about seven feet in height when alive, is now thought to be of Iron Age date, although the cremation was probably earlier. People believed the man must have been a Roman knight – hence the origin of the name Knightstone. However, although it was spelled Knightstone as long ago as 1758, it was more often written as Nightstone or Nitestone, and may have been a reference to the black appearance of the sea-drenched rock or the black marble that was quarried there and used for local fire surrounds.

As well as a bath house, Howe also constructed a lodging house, refreshment room and reading room on the island. Only the wealthy would have been able to afford to take the waters, since the cost of a hot salt-water bath was 3s, with a cold bath costing 1s. A labourer earned about 7s 6d a week at this time. Knightstone was still an island, and bathers were ferried over by local boatman, Aaron Fisher. This was clearly not an ideal situation and in 1824, when the baths were sold to the Reverend Thomas Pruen, a low causeway was built which allowed access by foot at low tide, although a boat was still required at high water.

In 1822 the first guide book for visitors to Weston was written. This gives us a delightful glimpse of the village as it was at that time. Then described as a 'fashionable summer retreat', it had a resident population of 735. Visitors could choose from a variety of accommodation including The Hotel, two inns and a number of private lodging houses. No one booked in advance, preferring to view prospective lodgings first. This could pose a problem in the height of the season. In 1826 Charlotte Wilson and her mother visited Weston whilst on holiday in Bath from London. They found that everywhere was full and, encumbered as they were with luggage and the stagecoach not returning until the next day, their situation was somewhat difficult. However, they were taken to see an old woman who, on hearing their predicament, exclaimed, 'Come all the way from Lunnon to Bath, and from Bath to Wesson! What wull 'em do? Here you Zue,' said the dame, 'Go wi' 'em to Varmer King's and ax him if he'd like to have 'em'. Sue took them

A self-portrait of Charlotte Wilson for her book The Old Farmhouse at Weston-super-Mare, *1826.*

to King's farmhouse in what is now Meadow Street where they settled in a 'whitewashed room in the farm, with a little casement window considerably lower than my head, and a door secured only by a wooden button'. On her return to London, Charlotte published a small book, illustrated by herself, about their experiences entitled *Somersetshire Dialogues or Reminiscences of The Old Farm House at Weston-super-Mare*, from which the above extracts are taken. In it she describes her visit and how she spent her time walking, sketching and learning the mysteries of making butter and cheese, once she had learned to understand the broad Somerset dialect! She described Weston as consisting of 'only four streets, two inns, and a few scattered houses, some of which had been newly built by the rustic inhabitants of Weston who, themselves, resided in small cottages with mould or stone floors'. She also recounted how Farmer King had another house on the beach, which he let out to visitors and how, in order to furnish it, he had virtually stripped the farmhouse of furniture and kitchen utensils!

Most holiday makers provided their own entertainment and when not 'taking the cure', would have read, walked and sketched. A favourite walk appears to have been up the hillside and out towards Worle, stopping at Lizzie Harris' tea gardens just on the brow of the hill at Milton where according to one diarist, visitors 'drank tea in her gay and beautiful flower garden and passed a very delightful hour at this sweet and retired spot.'

Blackberries grew in profusion in early autumn and town dwellers enjoyed the sights of 'rustic labourers busy with their team and plough' or listened to the 'Cottage Quoir of songsters', singing folk songs at the end of their working day. Crazes developed for collecting seaweeds, shells and fossils. These were then made into pictures and trinkets during the winter months, providing a souvenir of the holiday. There were two pleasure boats for hire and donkeys, or Jerusalem ponies as they were called locally, could be rented from fishermen for excursions to neighbouring villages and ancient sites. In 1836 W.T. Clark wrote in his diary:

> At about half past ten in the forenoon Mr Lawrence and I mounted on two stout and serviceable donkeys and set out for Locking, a distance of about 4 miles, and dismounting at the churchyard gate we sent our steeds with their attendants back to Weston...

Farmer King, drawn by Charlotte Wilson, 1826. Charlotte notes that he had lost the use of his left arm.

Dances were held at the Assembly Rooms, where residents and visitors alike danced until dawn, when the early morning light would have rendered it safe to return to their homes and lodgings without falling into the numerous streams and ditches that crisscrossed the village.

There was little to separate the beach from the village beyond an earth dyke with a walkway along the top. An entry in a diary written on a visit to Weston in August 1820 vividly describes this:

> In the evening we walked to the Beach, which was soon completely covered, never saw the tide more beautiful! No promenade was left for the company – drove up like a flock of sheep to the mounts at

Pencil drawing of cottages at Ashcombe, 1826. This is typical of the rural landscape that would have greeted visitors on their walks around the area at this time. (Collections of North Somerset Museum Service)

Watercolour of George Harse, donkey wheelchairman, c. 1852. George Harse was the son of one of the most notorious beerhouse keepers in Weston. He lived in Gas Street with his wife, two sons and three daughters. Next door was the George Inn where his father was landlord. George died in 1861, aged forty-two. (Collections of North Somerset Museum Service)

the edge of the Moor, gazing on the busy waves which hastily spread over the whole strand.

Clearly, an aspiring resort needed a promenade and in 1826 a surfaced walkway was built from Knightstone as far as Leeves' Cottage, extended three years later as far as Regent Street.

With the increasing numbers of visitors and residents alike, the small ancient parish church was no longer adequate, particularly during this period when almost everyone attended services. The building was Norman in origin but was remodelled some time in the fifteenth century. It was described by the Reverend John Collinson in his *History and Antiquities of the County of Somerset*, published in 1791, as 'a small building of one pace, eighty four feet in length and twenty in breadth, having at the west end a tower in which hang three bells'. The church was entered from the south, across a meadow and in through a porch in the centre of the nave. Rows of benches were laid across the nave, where the men sat towards the front and the women and children at the back. Until 1718 there was a small choir, but this was disbanded when singing in church was discouraged. Music was provided by

Early print of the original parish church. Top right is the silver chalice of 1573, lost in the early twentieth century.

a small orchestra playing a fiddle, flute and bassoon, the latter nicknamed by locals the 'horse's leg'. In the churchyard, the graves were edged with small stones and planted with sweet herbs, rosemary, thyme and fennel.

In 1804 George Bennett wrote that 'The roof and windows of the Church and Chancel are in a bad state of repair; one window in particular on the North side of the Chancel I observed to be much broken, and where the glass was wanting, its place supplied by bundles of hay'. The members of the vestry petitioned the rector, James Scott, to enlarge the church. However nothing was done, despite further petitions, until 1823, when the then rector and lord of the manor, Wadham Pigott, donated £1000 towards the project. By then the church was in such a poor state it was decided that rather than enlarge the existing church, they would demolish and rebuild it. The following year everything except the chancel was demolished. Most of the stone was reused, although many of the ancient stone carvings were thrown in a rubbish heap. A few locals took the more ornamental pieces for their gardens and some corbels (carved stone heads that supported roof timbers) can still be seen in gateways and around windows in houses nearby. The bells were removed and left in the churchyard. One villager remembered that, just after the bells had been removed and before demolition of the church began, they were propped up on timbers and struck by men with hammers to celebrate a wedding. Whilst the church was rebuilt, services were held in the parochial school room in Bristol Road which was reached up a lane and through a five-barred gate near the present YMCA. Part of the funding for the new church came from the purchase of private pews by wealthier residents and some lodging houses. In 1829 John Rutter wrote that 'most of the lodging houses have pews attached to them by purchase'. However, this practice was frowned upon by the Bishop and the rector was told to

One of the stone corbels from the original parish church. (Collections of North Somerset Museum Service)

The tower of the parish church today. You can still trace the two previous positions where the clock was sited. One is the large circle of lighter stone below the present position, and just below that again is a faint outline of curved stonework just over the porch.

put an end to it. In 1837, the Chancel was also rebuilt and a few years later the tower was raised with the addition of a fourth stage and the clock and bells moved up, so today very little remains of the original church. A few years after the new church opened, the old Norman font was recovered from a nearby field where it had been used as a cattle trough, and was reinstated in the church. The remnants of a thirteenth century churchyard cross stand by the south wall and a small stone relief carving can be seen inside the porch. These, together with the top of a small carved Norman window and some corbels in the collection of North

Somerset Museum Service are all that have survived today. The silver communion chalice of 1573 was lost in the early twentieth century.

Wadham Pigott died on Christmas Day 1823 and John Hugh Wadham Smyth Pigott became squire. Although Wadham was unmarried and childless, he did have an illegitimate niece, Anne Provis, who lived with him for many years. In 1815 she was married to the illegitimate son of Sir Hugh Smyth of Ashton Court, John Hugh Smyth, who was made heir on condition he assumed the name and arms of Pigott added to that of Smyth. John Hugh did much to improve Weston. He carried through the rebuilding of the church on Wadham's death and rebuilt and enlarged Grove House, adding an observatory to the grounds. One of his most public actions was the planting of Weston Woods in order to create a private game reserve with woodland walks. To involve the villagers, all the children were gathered together and each given a handful of seedlings and allocated a small plot into which to plant them. In fact, it took several attempts before the trees took hold in the shallow soil and exposed position, but they now form a picturesque backdrop to the town as well as a delightful place to walk, watch the wildlife and enjoy the views. At the same time a small gothic-style woodsman's cottage was built at the end of what is now Worlebury Hill Road. Today it is a private residence.

The town was growing apace now. The resident population in 1821 was 738, a huge increase from the 163 villagers of just ten years before. In 1830 a purpose-built reading and assembly rooms opened on the corner of Regent Street and the seafront. Run by Richard Hill, it boasted a library, reading and promenade room with a 'good collection of Books, periodicals and London Daily and Provincial papers'. The building still exists, incorporated into the Beach Hotel.

In 1828, Knightstone was sold to Dr Edward Long Fox of Bristol. Fox was a prominent Quaker physician with a particular interest in the

The woodsman's cottage, Worlebury Hill Road, c. 1907.

humane treatment of the insane. He felt that salt baths could help his patients both with physical and mental ailments. By now Fox was nearly seventy years old, but together with his son, Dr Francis Ker Fox, the pair set about developing the island further. In 1831, Reverend Skinner wrote in his diary that 'Many workmen are now engaged in levelling the surface of the Rock in order to make a courtyard or place of exercise for the patients.' Two years later the *Bristol Mirror* reported that 'Dr Fox of Brislington is engaged in erecting a spacious building on one Knightstone rock, at this place, for the purpose of introducing fresh and salt water, hot and cold vapour and shower, sulphur and every description of medicated baths'. Later the causeway was raised using Cornish granite, which was also used for the high, heavy walls protecting the island from the sea. Patients and visitors now had access on foot at any state of the tide. Contemporary reports state that Dr Fox spent over £20,000 on the improvements. In 1836, W.T. Clark visited Weston with his family, especially for his daughter to take the waters. He wrote in his diary:

Monday June 13th – Before breakfast Mr Lawrence and I walked to the Knightstone Baths where I had a cold shower for the second time, having commenced a series of seven baths on the Saturday preceding. Selina had a tepid bath at the same place at the temperature of 98° preparatory to bathing in the open sea which she is to begin to do daily on Wednesday.

Print of Regent Street, c. 1840. The building in the centre is the assembly rooms and library built by Richard Hill in 1830.

*Print of Knightstone
Baths, c. 1850.*

Selina probably just ducked under the water close to the beach, as was the custom. Bathing in the open sea could have its dangers. In 1824 a man died after being run through by a swordfish while swimming in Weston Bay!

There were other baths besides Knightstone. John Rutter, in his 1829 *Delineations of the County of Somerset* tells us that 'Near the Post Office, are other hot and cold plunging and shower baths, commodiously fitted up, under the superintendence of Mrs Jane Gill, one of the original bathing women of the place'. However, these did not have the luxury or facilities of Knightstone. One description tells us that the shower bath consisted of a man standing on a ladder to tip a bucket of water over the client!

The first post office was set up in Clarence House in Regent Street and run by Mrs Sawtell. Letters were carried by the local post carrier on his donkey, to catch the mail coach at the Churchill Turnpike, or later, at the coaching inn at Cross. Rutter wrote that 'the conveyance of letters to and from Weston loudly called for reformation. They are now from five to six hours coming from Bristol to Weston, and a London letter cannot at present be answered by return of post'. As late as 1843 there were still complaints of late deliveries, largely because the mail was still being brought by cart, rather than by the new railway.

By road, in 1822, Hawkin's coach took five hours to reach Weston from Bath. Ten years later a new coach, the *Hope*, started operating four days a week from 8.30 a.m. at the Plough Hotel to Bristol via Congresbury, Backwell and Brockley and returning at 4.15 p.m. However, there was no service from the Banwell and Langford area. Solitary visitors could ride or walk whilst wealthier tourists would probably possess their own coach. Travel was not without risk. In 1817, a newspaper report tells us that Harse & Hill's coach was being driven 'furiously' past the house of their rival operators in Congresbury, when it overturned, resulting in one passenger, Mrs Sheriff, being so badly bruised that 'her life is despaired of'.

MESSRS. HILL & HARSE beg leave to return their most sincere thanks to their Friends, the Nobility, Gentry, and Public in general, for the many favours bestowed upon them since their commencement of business as Coach Proprietors; and they also beg leave most respectfully to inform them that, on MONDAY NEXT, the 8th Instant they will commence running their

FOUR-HORSE COACH,
From the HOTEL,
WESTON-SUPER-MARE,

to the SWAN INN, BRIDGE STREET, BRISTOL, every Monday, Tuesday, Thursday, and Saturday, and to return on the Evenings of the same Days, (at 4 o'clock) during the Season. Every attention will be paid to the Comfort of those who may honour them with their favours.

Weston-super-Mare, June 5, 1818,

Advertisement for the coach service operated by Messrs Hill and Harse between Weston and Bristol, 1818.

Other dangers also lurked! In 1830 a grazier, Charles Hardwick, was attacked and badly wounded by a highwayman, again at Congresbury. In this instance the attacker, Richard Hewlett of Wick St Lawrence, was caught and hanged, but it is unlikely that it was an isolated instance. The opening of the railway in 1841 was therefore probably the single most important event in Weston's rise to popularity.

The main Bristol to Exeter railway bypassed the town by about 1½ miles to the south. The company had intended to run the line through Weston, but people were wary of having noisy, smelly steam engines in their smart growing resort – a decision they would come to regret in time! From the junction, a single-track branch line was laid into the town to a small station in what is now Alexandra Parade. In order to conform with the Great Western Railway from London to Bristol, the Bristol and Exeter Railway and the Weston branch line were built in Brunel's broad gauge of 7ft 0½in rather than the standard gauge of 4ft 8½in adopted elsewhere. Until 1851 the trains were drawn by horses. With a headwind it was said that this journey could take up to half an hour and that some passengers preferred to walk since it was quicker! In 1851 a steam engine was

Swiss Villa, from a print, c. 1852. The wagon and horses are being driven along Locking Road.

introduced and the journey from Junction to Town then only took about five minutes. Both stations were designed by Isambard K. Brunel, who is reputed to have stayed at Swiss Villa in Locking Road whilst overseeing construction of the local section. The following description was written in 1842 when Robert Smirke, architect of the British Museum, visited Weston with his sister, Mary, a talented artist:

> We arrived after a journey of 45 minutes at the Weston Junction, three miles from the Banwell Station, and eighteen and a half miles from Bristol. Here, leaving the train, we enter into carriages of a similar construction; but drawn by horses, who perform the distance, one mile and a quarter, on a branch line to Weston, in about ten minutes. The termination is at a good and well-built station, near the old turnpike road, at the eastern entrance to the town. In front of the building is an arcade, relieved by a projecting gable, with a carved finial and square turret and vane. At this station, it is well to add, tickets must be obtained on leaving Weston by rail, such not being issued at the junction.

Not everyone welcomed the new mode of travel, as Whereat's *New Handbook to Weston and its Vicinity* laments:

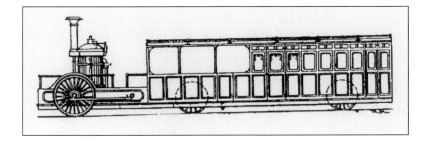

Fairfield, *the first steam engine and carriage to operate on the branch line between Weston Junction and Weston Town, 1851.*

...the opening of the Bristol & Exeter Railway....has rendered access to Weston an easy thing, compared with what it was before the days of railroad communication. Though we must hold to the importance of rapid locomotion, we cannot forget that there were pleasures connected with the old stage-coach style of travelling which are altogether lost in the modern mode of transit; and when whirled along express speed we catch a glance of some fair landscape instantly to lose it again, there steals over us a momentary regret that we cannot pull up to feast our eyes on the lovely spots we leave behind us in our journey.

Stagecoach services were withdrawn almost as soon as the railway opened.

The infrastructure for a town was growing and the same year that the railway arrived, a company was established to provide gas. A gas works was built in Oxford Street, opposite the end of High Street South, then called Gas Street, to supply fifty private consumers and forty-two public street lamps.

Weston officially became a town when, on 13 May 1842, the Improvement and Market Act was granted. This Act brought the local government of Weston-super-Mare under one authority, rather than the large number of different organisations previously responsible, among them the Diocese of Bath and Wells, the Churchwardens, the Manor and the Overseers of the Poor.

Eighteen local men volunteered to fill the new posts of Town Commissioners, the posts being subsequently filled by public election. The Commissioners held far-reaching powers to improve Weston, and brought in many of the local government controls we know today. For example, they could levy rates and borrow money for improvements. They could declare paths and streets public highways and acquire property and land by compulsory purchase order as long as it was for the benefit of the town. From this date, thatched roofs were banned on all new property; front doors had to open inwards so as not to knock down pedestrians when opened; gutters and down pipes from roofs became

compulsory so that people walking by would not get drenched by water from the roof. Bylaws were brought in to control and license hackney cabs, to attend to the welfare and control of animals and to prevent public nuisances. The Commissioners also took a lease on the new gas works, believing that this would enable them to provide street lighting in the most economical way. In fact, this proved not to be the case as the works were too small to cater for the needs of a growing town and the site allowed no room for expansion, so in 1851 the lease was terminated.

Law and order had been the responsibility of the parish constable, aided by concerned residents. In 1808, the Weston-super-Mare and Kewstoke Association was set up 'for the prevention of Depredation etc. and for the Prosecution of Offenders.' This was similar to other Associations in local villages, in which the larger land and property owners got together to ensure that any criminals were duly prosecuted. A parish stocks and whipping post stood in the churchyard, being moved when the church was rebuilt to a site in The Worthy at the bottom of Grove Park where the village lock-up stood. The Improvement Act set up Weston's first police constabulary, with a force of just two officers. This could pose a real problem when excursion trains brought 5000 or 6000 day trippers in a week, from St Philips, Bedminster and 'other disreputable neighbourhoods'! From reports and letters in the newspapers it was even felt that the future of Weston as a fashionable resort was at risk from this influx.

The Town Commissioners also built a new Market Hall at the north end of the High Street backing on to Worthy Lane, where the Playhouse stands today. A market had been held in the village since 1825. As well as garden produce, eggs and so on, livestock was slaughtered there and the fresh meat sold on the spot. The *Bristol Mirror* describes one occasion:

> In the meat market was a heifer, fed by J.B. Hellier Esq. of Wick St Lawrence, and slaughtered by Mr Ellis of Worle, and which, for symmetry of form when alive, and regularity of fat when dead, would not have been surpassed by any heifer ever seen at an agricultural meeting.

The new Hall enabled the commissioners to bring in hygiene controls and trading standards. An Inspector of Provisions kept an eye over the quality of produce and traders could be fined up to £5 for selling bad or unwholesome food. After the Market Hall was opened, animals could only be slaughtered at the new public abattoir.

The town finally got its own newspaper when, on 1 April 1843 James Dare published *The Westonian*, described as 'A monthly Arrival List and Directory for Weston-super-Mare and Journal of Local Intelligence, Advertisements, etc.'. Dare was a printer by trade but had gained

THE WESTONIAN;

A Monthly Arrival List

AND DIRECTORY FOR WESTON-SUPER-MARE,

AND JOURNAL OF LOCAL INTELLIGENCE, ADVERTISEMENTS, &c.

"To be or not to be, that is the question."—SHAKSPEARE.

No. 1.] SATURDAY, APRIL 1, 1843. [PRICE 2d.

OUR ADDRESS.

We have now put forth the first number of the *Westonian*, and we leave our readers to judge whether we have fulfilled all that the "Prospectus" promised, or whether we are to be included amongst Macbeth's "juggling fiends"

That keep the word of promise to the ear,
And break it to the hope.

"We trust there are none who will think so of us; but be that as it may, we feel it not only an absolute, but a most pleasing, duty, to return thanks to our subscribers for the success we have met with throughout our canvass—a success far exceeding our most sanguine expectations, and for which we can best shew our gratitude, by endeavouring to carry out fully, and faithfully, the terms of the "Prospectus."

But now let us protest (and we do so "more in sorrow than in anger") against the custom of prejudging works of the nature of the *Westonian*, which we regret to say we have, in one or two instances, met with.

An idea has somehow or other arisen, that this publication was to be conducted after the manner of a certain scandalous, and disgraceful pamphlet, which appeared some time back in Bath and Bristol, with the name of which we will not pollute our columns.—Now we do most solemnly deny any such intention—the sanctity of domestic privacy will never be invaded by us; we have too much regard for our own home, to make our paper subservient to the malignity of the slanderous, and too much hatred of such characters, to lend ourselves to those, whose only pleasure is in the real, or fancied, infirmities of their fellow-creatures.

Far, very far, from such an intention is ours; to quote our own "Prospectus," our object is "to render our little work of a *pacific, interesting*, and *useful* character, leaving to others the unenviable task of advocating the interests of polemical and speculative subjects."

We refer our readers confidently to the Directory, and other portions of the paper, feeling assured that we have, to the best of our ability, carried out our intentions.

Again to quote the "Prospectus," — "Abundant profession is always unadvisable;" we will only therefore add that our intention is to conduct the *Westonian* in strict adherence to the principles we have laid down; and we also hope that our readers will look upon this the first number with an indulgent eye; it will be our aim from time to time to supply a constant succession of original articles, which we trust will interest our readers, and we shall study so to frame every article in our little paper, that if its life should, despite of all our efforts, be limited to six months, there will not rise in judgment against us the recollection of

One line which *dying we could wish to blot.*

With another quotation from the "Prospectus," (varying it a little for present purposes) we shall now conclude: "the *Westonian* is before the public in April; and on its merits, not our promises, it must stand or fall."

WANTED TO PURCHASE,

A FEW BUSHELS OF CHOICE ENGLISH APPLES, viz.: The Nonpariel, Ribstone Pippen, Winter Pearmain, Pomeroy, Golden Pippen, Grumage or Stone Pippen, &c.
Apply at G. AFFLECK'S Fruit Shop, Weston-super-Mare.

BOOT & SHOE WAREHOUSE,
No. 5, High Street,

JAMES COLLINGS respectfully returns his sincere thanks and grateful acknowledgements to the Inhabitants and Visitors of Weston-super-Mare and its Vicinity, for their great patronage and support, and hopes, by a punctual attendance to business, added to reasonable charges, to ensure a continuance of the same.

A large assortment of ladies' and gentlemen's fashionable Boots, Shoes, and Slippers constantly on sale.

Ladies' fancy worked Slippers carefully made up.

ST. JAMES STREET, WESTON-SUPER-MARE.

JAMES BURGE,
(Late Foreman at Rumbach and Co.'s, London,)

TAILOR, DRAPER, HABIT AND PELISSE MAKER, in returning thanks for the unprecedented support he has received from the Gentry of this town and neighbourhood, begs to assure them, and the visitors and inhabitants generally, that all orders intrusted to him shall continue to be executed in a first-rate style of workmanship, at prices as low as at any other respectable establishment.

Broad Cloths, Kerseymeres, Waistcoatings, &c., in variety.—Gentlemen's own materials made up.

A Vacancy for an APPRENTICE, who would have every opportunity of acquiring a proficient knowledge of his business.

THE ART OF CUTTING, on the most scientific principles, TAUGHT in a few Lessons.

Front page of the first edition of The Westonian *newspaper, 1 April 1843.*

experience of newspapers while working in Bristol. He came to Weston and set up a small printing business before deciding to become a journalist. Newspapers were a risky business and few survived for any length of time. Aware of this James Dare wrote, on the front page of his fledgling paper, 'The Westonian is before the public in April, and on its merits, not our promises, it must stand or fall.' The people of Weston must have approved since it still flourishes over 150 years later, though now under the title *Weston & Somerset Mercury* and no longer under local ownership. It was not the only newspaper. Competition began in 1845 when the *Weston Gazette* was launched. Printed at the Mendip Press in Wadham Street, it again was a monthly periodical, although both papers became weekly in due course. The *Gazette* lasted until the 1950s, when it was bought out by the *Mercury*.

Glentworth Bay, c. 1852. The buildings shown are, from the left, Highcliff Lodge, Devonshire Cottage (now part of The Bayside Hotel), Villa Rosa, Princes and Albert Buildings.

The period saw increased development and, by 1838 when the Tithe Map was produced, Highcliff Lodge, Devonshire Cottage (now part of the Bayside Hotel), Coombe Bank and Park House had been built on the lower hillside. One of the more prominent mansions was the Italianate villa of local pink limestone built for Sophia Rooke in 1844. Villa Rosa, as it was named, was designed by Bath architect, James Wilson and built by Thomas Locock of Weston. One visitor was clearly overwhelmed by its beauty:

> But when in my rambles I beheld Villa Rosa, I rubbed my eyes as though awoke from a dream, Thinks I to myself, I am transported to the sweet south; I am traversing my beloved Appennines! So Italian, so happily situated, is this residence, but when I looked a little closer, I thought I espied some small architectural discrepancy; I doubted whether the crowning ornament of one of the turrets did not call me back to the English architecture of James or Elizabeth's reign. Be this as it may, there is so much good taste throughout, the grounds are so admirably disposed, and so liberally thrown open to the public, that if my criticism be correct – I vouch it not – it would be unfair to exercise it.

Villa Rosa formed the centrepiece of the first of the private estates. Gates and lodges were built at the entrance and both residents and non-residents had to pay to gain access. The fee for residents of the Villa Rosa estate was 15 shillings a year. Only the lower lodge survives today, together with the mansion's coach-house, now a private residence called Villa Rosetta, the ornamental bridge that linked the two parts of the villa's garden over Shrubbery Road, and the pumping tower Miss Rooke built to provide water to the estate. This was in use until 1890 when the local authority laid on mains water.

Next came one of Weston's finest developments – Royal Crescent. Built in 1847, it was designed to imitate those at Bath and, together with Park Place and Greenfield Place, formed an elegant square around a private garden leading down to the promenade and beach. Oriel Terrace, next to the parish church, was also built that year. Whereat's *New Handbook* described it as 'built in the Elizabethan style, and the several tenements being combined in one frontage, the façade presents a very imposing spectacle. They are separated from the road by pretty little lawns bordered with flowers and altogether have an appearance both of neatness and comfort'.

Early education in Weston-super-Mare, as in most places, relied on private or charitable institutions. The first school in Weston opened in 1702 and was paid for by the parish who employed a local woman, Elizabeth Barber, to teach basic reading and writing skills. As Weston grew, so more schools opened, especially private boarding schools for the children of the gentry. John Rutter mentions a Sunday school under the direction of the Revd Jenkins as well as 'several respectable seminaries for young gentleman and ladies in this healthy and convenient bathing place'. Sunday schools of this date did not just teach religion but basic reading, writing and arithmetic, and were held on this day as it was the only free day for those children, and adults, who worked the rest of the week. In 1845 the National School, run by the Church of England, was built at the corner of Lower Church Road and Knightstone Road. In an appeal for funds the *Gazette* wrote:

So many boys flock to Weston from all parts of the country and have constant employment during the short season, but are left

Lower Church Road, c. 1850. The National School, pictured here in the foreground, was demolished when Weston Technical College was built in 1969.

with no resource throughout the long wintry months except the casual charity of the resident... In the hope, therefore, that our wealthy visitants may feel the importance of imparting to these youths thus thrown adrift upon the world, the advantages of a sound religious education, as the means of regulating their future life and making them moral and useful members of society, we are tempted to raise our humble voice in the furtherance of the welfare of this institution.

Later the British School opened in Hopkins Street for the children of non-conformists.

Religion was still very much part of everyday life and the increasing population called for additional places of worship. In October 1847 Emmanuel church was built in Oxford Street, to serve the artisans and shopkeepers living and working in the cluster of new streets in the southern half of the town. Other denominations made do with converted houses until congregations were large enough to fund a purpose-built church. The Roman Catholics for example, met in a room at the Railway Hotel until 1858 when St Joseph's church was built in Camp Road. When Methodism arrived in Weston in 1791, the year of John Wesley's death, its followers met in a cottage. The first independent chapel came many years later, and is now the Regent Street branch of Barclay's Bank.

In January 1848 work started for John Hugh Smyth Pigott on cutting the Toll Road along the northern side of Worle Hill from Birnbeck to Kewstoke. Tolls were initially 6d for a two-horse carriage, 3d for a horse and 1d for a donkey chair. However, pedestrians were never charged since the road followed an ancient public footpath, which led to the Mulpit Stone near the shore at Sand Bay, the boundary of the Manor of Weston. John Hugh was particularly proud of his new road and used to keep flower seeds in his pockets, which he scattered on the banks whenever he rode along it. In summer the air was full of scent and bright with colour.

Once open, the new road encouraged more traffic through the Claremont area and it must have been about this time that one of the few remaining reminders of village Weston was demolished – Billy Board's cottage. This was described in *Browns Guide* as a 'Quaint old lodge overspread with ivy and honeysuckle, and protected by the rocky hill, with its blooming ferns and waving brushwood.' It stood at the entrance to the West Field, an area of common grazing land and was home to Billy Board, who was Weston's oldest resident when he died in 1861 aged eighty-eight. Victoria Crescent in Madeira Road was built first, followed by Wellington Terrace, both designed by a London architect, William Christie. Both the Claremont Hotel and the Royal Pier Hotel were erected in 1854. Although the latter was built as a hotel, it began life as

Advertisement for the Royal Claremont Pier Hotel, 1872.

Anchor Head School, run by Dr Godfrey before being returned to its original purpose about 1872. The following years saw the shaping of the Claremont area as it is known today as marine villas were gradually built all along Birnbeck Road. The next fifty years would see the town double in size again.

CHAPTER 5
Resort to Town

In the second half of the nineteenth century the town began to take shape. South Road, Atlantic Terrace, Ellenborough Crescent and the Boulevard were among the roads completed at this time. The larger villas attracted upper middle class families such as East India Company merchants, surgeons, clergymen and retired military officers, men like George Day VC. George Fiott Day was a naval officer who fought during the Crimean War. Alone and at night he crossed into enemy lines to survey and report on the enemy's ships. For his courageous action he won the Victoria Cross and Bar. He retired to Claremont Crescent, Weston, dying there in 1876. Houses of this size required a large establishment of staff to run them, and often had separate stable blocks and coach houses. A photograph of staff at Seafield, South Road, in about 1900, shows two parlourmaids, two gardeners, two coachmen, a housekeeper, cook and lady's maid.

The lord of the manor still held the majority of the land, which was gradually released for development. He therefore had a vested interest in creating a pleasant and desirable environment. Much of the day to day responsibility for this rested in his land agent, Robert Landemann Jones. One reason that Victorian Weston is so harmonious with the landscape is

Staff at Seafield, South Road, Weston, c. 1900. In the back row from left to right are the parlourmaid, under-gardener, head coachman, another parlourmaid, head gardener Mr Daffern, housekeeper and under-coachman. In the front row are the cook and lady's maid.

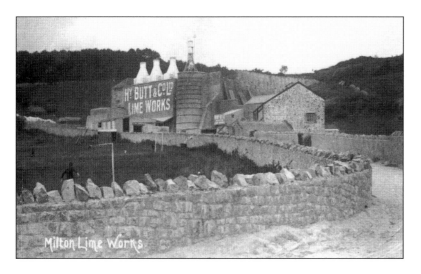

Milton Quarry and Lime Works, c. 1907.

that most of the new villas were built from local limestone, quarried from the hillside. Small quarries can still be traced along the slopes, such as in Atlantic Road, but the main source of stone was the Town Quarry at the top of Queens Road. Quarrying here began some time before 1815 continuing until 1953. In the Weston-super-Mare Enclosure Award it was listed as the 'parish quarry' where stone could be taken for local roads. In addition, owners and tenants of the auster tenements were free to quarry stone for their own purposes. In 1875 there were 200 people claiming such rights until they were gradually bought out by the Local Authority.

In the 1850s what became Weston's largest quarry opened at Milton. In the mid-1880s it was taken over by Henry Butt, a local entrepreneur, and over the next fifty years was extended eastwards for nearly half a mile. Lime, for mortar and plaster among other uses, was produced at all Weston's quarries, but until 1939, Butt's Quarry was the biggest producer of white lime in the west of England, even exporting it abroad.

In fact most of Weston's older buildings were made entirely from local resources. The limestone exteriors masked interior walls built from bricks. These were made in huge numbers at the Royal and Original Potteries in Locking Road, which also produced chimney pots, drains, and a variety of roofing tiles. The Potteries were one of Weston's most successful businesses. Established as two separate works in the 1840s, they later merged to become the town's biggest industry aside from tourism, employing hundreds of men. By the 1850s both works had diversified into flowerpots and garden statuary which was exported all over the world, although bricks and tiles always formed the basis of production. The pottery remained in production until 1961, when labour shortages and the development of the plastic flowerpot forced its closure.

Ironwork and street furniture was also made in the town. H. Pond

Cast-iron drain grille made at Hillman's Iron Foundry, Richmond Street, Weston.

Parties are requested to observe, when making purchases, that they are dealing at

PHILLIPS' WESTON-SUPER-MARE POTTERY.

CHIMNEY POTS—Please observe that 20 different sizes and patterns of Chimney Tops, are manufactured at

PHILLIPS'S POTTERY,

at prices varying from 1s. 6d. to 10s. 6d each. Any other description made to order. The above may be had either red dun, black glazed, or freestone colour, at corresponding prices.

ARCHITECTS and BUILDERS can be supplied with any kind of Crease Tiles, according to pattern and pitch. The usual length is about 18 inches, but for large public buildings they can be made of greater length and proportionate size, coloured if required. Plain and Double Roman Tiles to match. Single Channel and Plain ditto; Hollow and Solid Bricks; Gutter ditto, and Paving Squares, of different sizes, manufactured at PHILLIPS'S POTTERY.

ALL sized SOCKET PIPES, in two feet lengths, glazed or plain, made at PHILLIPS'S POTTERY from two inches to 16 inches in diameter. The glaze is warranted to stand, it being composed of lead ore, and burnt into the Pipes. They can be manufactured of any pattern. Pipes of similar make supplied for Flues, and instructions sent for using the same, on application at PHILLIPS'S POTTERY, Land Drain Pipes of all sizes in 12-inch lengths.

C. PHILLIPS, Sen., Proprietor of the above Manufactory, having had 45 years' practical experience in the business, can with confidence assure the public that no Manufacturer in England can possibly excel him in producing superior goods in either department. Price Lists on application.

Sole Agent in Weston and its Neighbourhood for RICH'S much approved STONE WARE PIPES.

A Book of Drawings of a number of Articles manufactured at Phillips' Pottery forwarded on application.

C. P. begs to remind his patrons and the Public in general, that the above manufactory is under his sole personal superintendence; that he has no Depot in any other Town, that he employs no Traveller or Agent, and would therefore request that all communications be made direct to him at the above address.

A page from Beedle's Guide to Weston-super-Mare, advertising some of the products made at Charles Phillips' Royal Pottery, c. 1860.

established an iron foundry in Richmond Street in 1840. Ten years later it was taken over by William Hillman and remained in operation until the 1960s. A description of the firm in a 'Where to Buy' booklet of 1890, stated that 'being the only iron founders in the town, they have taken an active share in the development of the town itself, as regards supplying private and public buildings and places with railings, gates, machinery and other goods they make'. Hillman's not only made their own branded goods, but would produce for local builders and firms such as the Weston Gaslight Company. Manhole covers and drain grills marked Addicott and Stradling, the names of two local building firms, are particularly common.

Probably the one person who has contributed most to the look of Victorian Weston was the architect Hans Fowler Price. Price was born in Bristol in 1835, and trained under T.D. Barry of Liverpool. He married Jane Baker, the daughter of the solicitor to the Smyth Pigott estate, and they moved to Weston. In 1876, Price was joined by a partner, Mr Wooler. Wooler was also a competent and imaginative architect and it is interesting that many of the buildings attributed to Hans Price were often the work of his partner. Wooler visited Spain in the 1870s and was very taken by the Moorish architecture, resolving to use some of the features in the first commission he obtained back in Weston-super-Mare. These were two villas at the top of Grove Park. You can still see today the typical Moorish ogee-shaped windows and the rows of ceramic tiles that Wooler imported from Spain. The houses are unique in Weston. It was also in Spain that Wooler saw the cathedral of Saragossa, which is said to have inspired the design for the offices of the local newspaper, the *Weston Mercury and Somerset Herald*, built in 1885.

The last traces of village Weston were now somewhat of an anachronism. Brown's *New Guide for Visitors*, written in 1854, believed Leeves' Cottage could not long survive:

Hans Fowler Price, architect of many of Weston's Victorian buildings.

Numbers 83 and 85 Grove Park Road. These villas were designed by Hans Price's partner, Mr Wooler. They show a distinct Moorish influence, inspired by his visit to Spain in the 1870s.

Recently the appearance of the cottage has suffered greatly from innovation. The lawn or foreground was wont to be tastefully ornamented with rockwork and flowers and shrubs of various kinds. Attached was a stable, equally rustic and picturesque, which is now replaced by a handsome dwelling house (Victoria Hall).

This makes it all the more surprising that part of the cottage can still be seen today, as the Thatched Cottage Restaurant.

The increasing number of residents, 4033 in the 1851 census, doubling to over 8000 by 1861, had filled the old burial ground around the parish church. The Town Commissioners chose a new site for a public cemetery, on the southern side of Bristol Road, on what were then the outskirts of Weston. The design was put out to tender and was won by Bath architect, Charles Davis. The cemetery included two mortuary chapels, one Church of England and one Nonconformist, and an arboretum of native and exotic trees. Many of these trees can still be seen, including Atlas cedar, Stone pine, Lucombe oak and two renowned monkey puzzles or Chilean pines. When the cemetery opened in 1856 the local churchyards were closed to new burials. Interestingly, the Commissioners chose the same site that Bronze Age people used to bury their dead, and broken remains of funerary urns were often uncovered by gravediggers. In the 1930s, the cemetery was enlarged by extending it down to Milton Road but it too is now full and today the deceased are interred at the Ebdon Road cemetery at the crematorium at Worle.

Until now people had relied on private wells, springs and rainwater cisterns for their water. Early advertisements for building plots often included the fact that fresh water was available on site. The problem with this was that sewage was usually discharged directly into the streams and rhynes and pollution and disease became a real risk. The first sewers were laid from the 1840s onwards, but construction could not keep up with the development of the town so the Commissioners employed Sir Joseph Bazalgette, the engineer responsible for London's sewers, to design a new system, which was completed in 1866. Whilst many homes continued to rely on wells, a waterworks was built in 1853 to supply domestic properties in the lower part of the town. The main supply came from a spring at Ashcombe, and a pumping station was built on site. One effect of the new facility was that some residents could now install fountains in their gardens and the Royal Pottery developed a number of elaborate designs, though not one surviving example has yet been discovered.

A new gas works was completed in 1856. The number of street lamps had by then more than doubled, and was increasing every year, as were the numbers of domestic customers, and the small works in Oxford Street could no longer cope with demand. A site was chosen in Drove Road for

One of several designs of terracotta fountain, from a Royal Pottery catalogue, c. 1872.

the new works, which were designed by E.W. Cowper of Westminster. Coal was brought in both by rail and by sea from Wales into Knightstone Harbour. Production stopped at Weston-super-Mare in 1968, but a small gas plant was retained on a standby basis for a short period and the gas-holders are still used for storage.

A collier unloading at Knightstone Harbour, c. 1900.

When the Town Commissioners were first formed, they met in a variety of hired rooms, among them the Plough Hotel in the High Street. However, some believed it gave the wrong impression to be meeting in a pub and that permanent offices were needed. A local speculative developer, Henry Davies, offered to build a town hall at his own expense, but the Commissioners suspected his motives. Davies had recently acquired the Whitecross Estate, directly adjoining the site chosen for the town hall, and people thought he might be trying to enhance its value. The issue was resolved when Archdeacon Henry Law, a former rector of Weston and generous benefactor of the town, purchased the building and donated it to the people of Weston. Constructed in 1858, it was designed by James Wilson, the architect responsible for Villa Rosa, and built by local builder, John Perry. As well as meeting rooms and a large council chamber, the building also incorporated a police station and cells, and offices for the Magistrates' Clerk, Town Surveyor and accountants.

The majority of visitors still travelled by train, into the tiny single-track terminus now twenty years old. Goods traffic had increased

The town hall and Emmanuel church, from a print of 1861.

When a new railway station was built in 1866, the line was made double-track. This signal box was built at this time. It can still be seen close to the present station, but aligned to the original broad-gauge branch line from Weston Junction to Weston Town.

greatly and better facilities were essential. In 1861 a separate Goods Station was built in a field in front of Whitecross House. One of the first people to take advantage was Charles Phillips, owner of the Royal Pottery, who sent out three wagon-loads of flower pots. An example of how much markets were opened up by the railway is illustrated by the fact that in 1867, a Liverpool wholesaler advertised in the *Weston Mercury* for local growers willing to supply and ship weekly consignments of local garden produce.

Five years later a new passenger station was built and an additional line laid along the branch. By relocating the new station across the road from the original site, it did away with the need for a level crossing over Locking Road, which had been a major nuisance for road travellers and the scene of many accidents. The new station had two platforms, a separate excursion platform and a refreshment hall where tea could be bought at 1½ d a cup or made from your own ingredients. Because the new station was still at the end of a branch line the situation was not ideal but it made it easier to deal with the growing influx of tourists. The Junction Station was the major problem now. Built on the moor, it exposed passengers and their luggage to rain and wind. The Revd Jackson, in his *Visitor's Handbook to Weston and its Vicinity*, wrote:

In all probability, even if a village be the object of approach, the stage coach of our fathers has been superseded by the rail. Weston for the last thirty years has thus been approached…At Weston Junction the traveller changes trains, and as he traverses the remaining mile and a half, he may readily observe the place of his destination…The Station itself is thoroughly well arranged, and

Romano-British enamelled brooch, found in South Terrace in 1959 during the digging of a drainage pit. (Collections of North Somerset Museum Service)

Watercolour of Knightstone, 1820. Howe's Baths opened on Knightstone Island in July 1820. Knightstone was still an island and visitors had to be ferried over by local boatmen until a low causeway was built four years later. (Collections of North Somerset Museum Service)

Portrait of Colonel John Pigott. After inheriting the Manor of Brockley from his father, Colonel Thomas Pigott, John bought the Manors of Ashcombe and Weston-super-Mare in 1695, building Grove House as a holiday cottage. (Collections of North Somerset Museum Service)

Dr Fox's Bath House. Dr Fox bought Knightstone in 1828 and, together with his son, developed the island further, building this Bath House in 1832. As this photograph shows, it has recently undergone restoration, although it is still awaiting a tenant.

Watercolour of the first railway station at Weston by W.R. Crotch, 1844. This building was designed by Brunel, as was the Junction station at the other end of the branch line. The wagon of hay on the right was to feed the horses that, for the first ten years, drew the trains. Behind the station clock tower is the Railway Hotel, which today is Jack Stamp's beerhouse. (Collections of North Somerset Museum Service)

Watercolour of the ladies' bathing place, Anchor Head, by Mary Smirke, 1842. Mary was the sister of the architect Robert Smirke, who designed the British Museum. This painting is one of eleven watercolours Mary painted during a family holiday at Weston, when she was sixty-three years old. (Collections of North Somerset Museum Service)

Print of Weston from the hillside, c. 1842. The parish church is on the left, with Knightstone Baths to the right. The hillside is largely undeveloped, while the area around St James Street, Carlton Street and Oxford Street is beginning to fill up. In the distance, two steam trains can be seen on the main line.

Mrs Sawtell's clock. Made by Bartlett of Bristol, it hung in the first post office, where Mrs Sawtell was postmistress. (Collections of North Somerset Museum Service)

Watercolour of Lizzie Harris, aged ninety-two, in 1852. Elizabeth Harris was the widow of an agricultural labourer. In the 1830s she opened the Milton Hill Tea Gardens where visitors 'drank tea in her gay and beautiful flower garden and passed a very delightful hour at this sweet and retired spot'. She died in 1855. (Collections of North Somerset Museum Service)

Victoria Buildings, Knightstone Road, 2002. Most of this terrace has been converted into hotels with extra storeys added to the top floor. This is the last house that remains much as it was built in the late 1830s.

Oil painting of Weston Sands by W.H. Hopkins, c. 1860. The artist's viewpoint is roughly where the entrance to the Grand Pier is today. The buildings on Beach Road end with Etonhurst. (Collections of North Somerset Museum Service)

A printed souvenir of Weston, late 1860s. It is double-sided, opening out like a flower, and shows sixteen different views of the town.

Anchor Head and Claremont, 2002. Today this cove is a favourite sunbathing spot. Above the beach is the back of the Royal Pier Hotel. The original building of 1854 is the centre section, later extended to the right and then to the left. In the distance is Birnbeck Pier.

Shrubbery Bridge. This was built in the 1850s to link the two parts of the garden of Villa Rosa. Shrubbery Road runs underneath.

Many of Weston's buildings have attractive architectural details such as carved figures and datestones. This piece of stained glass is a reminder of the original use of one of the amusement arcades in Regent Street.

Now a betting office and night club, this was the original Atlantic Cable Office in Richmond Street. Opposite was Hillman's iron foundry.

Wadham Street Garage. This was one of Weston's earliest motor garages, opening in 1912. The red-brick building next door is Weston Heritage Centre.

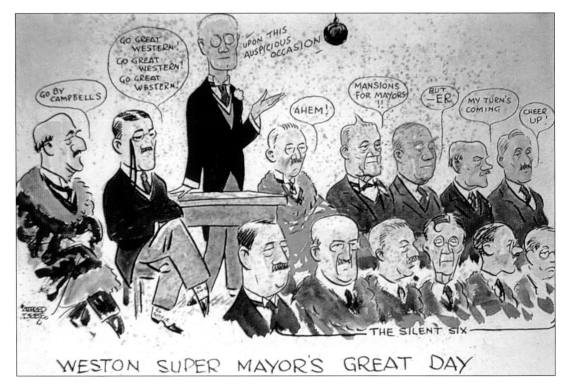

Cartoon by Alfred Leete, commemorating the opening of the Winter Gardens in 1927. The figures depicted are, from left to right, the Mayor of Cardiff, Ernest Palmer (vice-chairman of the GWR), T. Macfarlane, the Lord Mayor of Bristol, Henry Butt, Barney Butter, William Wilcox and Sydney Smith. (Collections of North Somerset Museum Service)

Leavers' ironmongers was founded in 1886 in Meadow Street, Weston. Mr Leaver went into partnership with the Fox brothers in 1894, with the business becoming J.J. Leaver in 1905. They moved to the High Street in 1939 and then to Waterloo Street where the business is carried on today by J.J.'s grandson, Roger Leaver.

Cover of the 1938 Town Guide, illustrating the open-air pool with its once-famous diving boards.

View over the town from Shrubbery Road, early 1980s. The tower of the parish church is in the centre while in the distance to the left is the spire of Christ Church. Although the outward sprawl has continued, this photograph was taken before the huge out-of-town retail developments at Winterstoke Road.

The Lily Pond, Winter Gardens, Spring 2002. The two ducks are now regular visitors, bringing up their family each year before flying off for the winter. On the left are some of the conference suites built in 1992, whilst in the centre is the Sovereign Shopping Centre.

Marine Lake, showing the 1885 sea walls. When the Marine Lake was built, the promenade was extended out over the lake with a colonnaded walkway underneath. This suffered in the 1981 gale to the extent that it had to be demolished.

Rossiter's jewellers was founded in 1832 by John R. Rossiter, as a watch and clockmakers and silversmiths. A second shop opened in Clevedon in 1892 and they now have four shops with one in Bridgwater and another in Barnstaple. The photograph shows the Weston shop in 2000, with the two youngest Rossiter brothers.

Grand Pier pavilion. This opened in 1933, replacing the Edwardian one destroyed by fire. The glazed shelter down the centre of the pier was added in 1927.

Weston promenade the morning after the great gale of December 1981. Westerly gales combined with very high tides caused great destruction and flooding all along the seafront.

Jill's Garden, Grove Park. This was created in July 2001, as a tribute to Jill Dando, the television presenter who grew up in Weston, and who was murdered on her doorstep in London in 1999. The garden was created by the BBC Ground Force team in just three days. The blue colour was chosen to represent the forget-me-not, Jill's flower.

The post of Town Crier was first established in Weston in the 1850s. There have been six official holders of the position – George Reed, Emmanuel Harvey, Edward Pavey, Charles Wilkins, William Davis and George Comer. In 1991 the post was revived as a ceremonial one, with the appointment of Brian 'Pluto' Venn. He has won many trophies including World Champion Town Crier.

Weston has always been renowned for the beauty of its sunsets.

Some things at the seaside never change, as this shop in Oxford Street shows. Buckets and spades for the beach and postcards to send home have been bought since the late nineteenth century.

managed with a genial attention to the wants and reasonable wishes of visitors. It must be regretted that the Junction shed often fails of affording adequate protection to the luggage of travellers. It was built at a time when trains were shorter than at present, a circumstance which explains the result, but does not effectually console the owner of wetted boxes and portmanteaux.

During this period the hillside became one large building site. On a map of 1854, only the large villas lining Birnbeck Road were built, together with those in Kewstoke Road and the western end of South Road. By the 1860s much of what became known as Cliftonville was complete, including Atlantic Road with its terraces and central church of Holy Trinity, Paragon Road, the eastern half of South Road, Highbury Road and Upper Church Road. The first building took place in Upper Church Road in the 1850s on the southern side. In 1855, during the Crimean War, Raglan Circus was in the process of being built when news arrived that the body of the Allied Commander, Lord Raglan, was to be brought up the Bristol Channel by boat that day. To mark that event, the name Raglan Circus was chosen. The central area behind the buildings, now a car park, was laid out as a private pleasure garden for the circus, with a small summer house in the centre.

In the mid-1860s Weston nearly became a terminus, or at least the nearest stopover, for New York bound steamships! As early as 1841 a Captain Evans was extolling the advantages of Brean Down as a deep sea harbour and packet station. However, it was not until twenty years later that the Brean Down Harbour and Railway Act officially passed through Parliament. It was intended to build a railway from the Bristol and Exeter

The proposed Brean Down Harbour Scheme of 1864.

main line, through a tunnel in the Down to three large docks. The foundation stone was laid on 5 November 1864. However, as the tide rose, the stone drifted off towards Steep Holm. Undeterred, the builders pressed on but were continually beset with problems. Over the winter, storms wrought havoc on the harbour, wrecking it completely in 1872 when the idea was finally abandoned.

While the main attractions of a seaside resort were complete, there was one major feature still lacking – a pier. Although there had been earlier attempts to construct a pleasure pier, notably Mr Dredge's suspension bridge scheme in 1845, nothing more had been done since that failed. With the second highest tidal range in the world, the Bristol Channel is particularly unforgiving in attempts to tame it. The site for Dredge's pier had been chosen to link the tiny islet of Birnbeck with the mainland below Worlebury Hillfort and it was here that a new pier was planned. Eugenius Birch was chosen as engineer. Birch was a renowned expert, being to piers what Brunel was to railways. He designed a cantilever construction, which was assembled from prefabricated cast iron, made at the Isca iron foundry in Newport, Wales. Birnbeck Pier opened in 1867, attracting 120,000 people in the first three months. A

Birnbeck Pier, from a print of 1870. The steamer jetty at this date was aligned with the rest of the pier. The present jetty was not built until 1872, when this one was removed.

pleasure pier enabled a person to walk out to sea and enjoy the bracing air and fine views, unhindered by any thoughts of seasickness or of sinking. However, piers also provided ideal berths for pleasure boats. From 1825 steamers had been taking passengers on occasional trips down the Channel picking them up from a wooden jetty at Knightstone. The first regular sailings to and from Weston began in 1860 and proved so popular that on 29 June 1861, over 700 excursionists arrived from Wales. The pier allowed further expansion of steamer services and in 1872 another jetty was built on its southern side, allowing boats to berth even at low water.

Throughout the second half of the nineteenth century the cultural life of the town flourished. The Smyth Pigotts moved in high social circles and many famous visitors stayed with them at Grove House. The writer Wilkie Collins, best known for his novel *The Woman in White*, stayed with Dr Stringfield at Verandah House, after which he wrote *The Voyage of the Tomtit*, based on an actual trip from Weston to the Isles of Scilly. Celebrated musicians played to packed houses at the Assembly Rooms – men such as Henryk Wieniavsky, the Polish composer and violinist, and pianist Sigismund Thalberg, who in the 1860s was as famous as Liszt as a performer. This trend continued well into the 1930s, with the Grand Pier pavilion and Winter Gardens hosting world-class classical musicians and singers. In 1937 a concert by the Ukrainian pianist Pouishnoff, broadcast live on radio, was heralded as 'the greatest concert in Winter Gardens' history'.

The town's foundations as a resort were not forgotten and bathing remained the chief reason for visiting the seaside. The Bylaws still insisted people used bathing machines, requiring those intended for use by the different sexes to be kept at least 200 yards apart and that boats should be kept the same distance away. Not everyone obeyed, however.

In 1872 the Revd Kilvert described his visit to Weston in his diary:

It seemed rather absurd to employ a man, a horse and a great house on wheels to enable a British human creature to dip himself in the sea.

Wednesday 4th September. Bathing in the morning before Breakfast from a machine. Many people were openly stripping on the sands a little further on and running down into the sea, and I would have done the same but I brought no towels of my own.

Thursday 5th September. I was out early before breakfast this morning bathing from the sands. There was a delicious feeling of freedom in stripping in the open air and running down naked to the sea, where the waves were curling white with foam and the red morning sunshine glowing upon the naked limbs of the bathers.

Glentworth Bay and the ladies' bathing machines, c. 1890.

Donkeys were a well-established beach attraction now and, in addition to the animals being ridden, they also pulled small carriages or donkey chairs. These were similar to bath chairs, drawn by one donkey, with the driver, known as a donkey wheelchairman, running alongside. They appear to have been more or less unique to Weston and were used as a form of taxi, taking people all around the town. They remained in use up to the 1920s and a surviving example can be seen at North Somerset Museum in Weston. Of all seaside resorts, Weston is probably associated most with donkeys. Over the years even the postman and town crier rode them and in the 1960s a cartoon version called 'Sunny' was used on all the town's publicity.

Two major investments in the town's health needs were made during this period. In 1865 a small hospital was built in Alfred Street. Before this opened, people had to be treated at home by local doctors, however serious their injury or illness. A few years later, an old pub called the Halfway House, at the southern end of the seafront, was converted into a small sanatorium for people recovering from illness or accident and who it was felt would benefit from sea air and bathing. It was funded by endowments, private donations and the small weekly payments made by patients. It proved so popular that in 1871 the foundation stone was laid for a new building. Named the West of England Sanatorium, patients had the use of a glazed conservatory, chapel and, from 1890, an indoor

swimming pool. In later years it was taken over as an extension for Weston Hospital, before becoming redundant when the new hospital was opened at Uphill in 1986. Today the building has been converted into private apartments under the name Royal Sands.

Weston was about to enter its heyday.

The Royal West of England Sanatorium, c. 1910. It was converted into private apartments in the 1990s and is now called Royal Sands.

CHAPTER 6
Weston's Heyday

The most important development at the end of the nineteenth century was the Seafront Improvement Scheme. The earlier promenades provided a seafront walkway but no protection from the sea, which regularly flooded streets and shops. This ambitious project, which took three years to complete, raised and levelled the promenade from the Sanatorium to Birnbeck Pier, creating the seafront roadway and removing the last remaining area of natural beach, at Glentworth Bay.

The second most significant development at the time was that Weston finally got a through railway station, when a loop off the main line was laid into the town. Built in standard gauge only, no broad gauge trains could use the loop line although they still continued on the main line until 1892, when broad gauge was abandoned throughout the whole country. The branch line was lifted and Weston Junction station demolished. You can still trace the line of the branch as Winterstoke Road runs along most of its length until the major roundabout close to Asda. The short road off to the left from the second roundabout by Blockbuster is called Old Junction Road. For a while the old town station was used for band concerts before being converted for use as a larger goods station. It remained as such until 1966, despite severe bomb damage during the Second World War. Tesco's supermarket now occupies this site.

People still normally waited until arrival before looking for somewhere

The railway station, c. 1910. This was Weston's third railway station, opening in 1884 and still in use today.

to stay. At the station, the drivers of the wagonettes and the porters would know where lodgings could be had, or visitors could ask at Whereat's Library, where a list was kept. The *Visitor's Handbook* of 1877 wrote that 'Most people choose to devote their first hours to selecting the house or rooms in which they are about to take up their abode. In this case they have to go through the troublesome ceremony of a lodging-hunt before they taste any of the enjoyments in store for them... Every intelligent hirer of a house or lodging is tolerably sure to make some inquiries regarding drains'. Bylaws were strict regarding boarding houses. The windows of every bedroom were to be kept open from 9 a.m. to 11 a.m. and from 2 p.m. to 4 p.m. unless prevented by stormy weather. There was a wide variety of accommodation from which to choose, from the largest hotels such as the Grand Atlantic or Royal Pier to small private boarding houses in Weston's back streets.

The town now welcomed many thousands of visitors, a high proportion of them day trippers on Bank Holiday excursions and works outings. As the numbers had increased, so the class of visitor changed. By the 1900s some low-paid workers such as office staff, shop assistants and some factory workers were getting holidays with pay. For many resorts, Weston-super-Mare included, this trade became the mainstay of their custom. However, whereas the early visitors had been content to make their own entertainment, these new arrivals wanted more fun laid on. This was the era of the band, the concert party, pierrots and funfair rides. New shops opened and the High Street took on the role it maintains today. In 1900 the Royal Arcade was built. This provided an additional covered shopping area and linked the High Street with Regent Street and the sea front, much as the Sovereign Shopping Centre does today. It remained a popular mixture of tea rooms, toy and souvenir shops until much of it was

This was the last remaining part of the Royal Arcade in 1990. It ran from Cecil Walker's shop in Post Office Road to the back of Marks and Spencer's. In the picture the shops are empty prior to demolition for the Sovereign Shopping Centre.

demolished in 1939. The last remaining section, from Cecil Walker's menswear shop to the back of Marks & Spencer, was pulled down in 1992. Service industries also grew. In this respect Milton became very important. Not only was it the market garden of the town, supplying fresh fruit and vegetables to shops and hotels, but the women offered laundry services for residents, hotels and their guests. It became a common sight to see the underwear of the ladies of Weston, displayed for all to see, as they were spread out on bushes and lines to dry!

Sport was becoming part of everyday life for more and more people and many of Weston's clubs were founded at this time, including those for cricket, football, golf and bowling. Weston-super-Mare Cycling Club was founded in 1878 during a country-wide craze for the new activity. An 1889 advertisement described Weston as having 'the best Cycling Track in England', in the Recreation Ground in Drove Road. Another sport for which Weston became world famous was water polo. In 1896 the Local Authority bought Knightstone, in order to build much-needed new holiday amenities. All the existing buildings were demolished, with the exception of Dr Fox's Bath House. The land area was then extended by erecting girders over an earlier swimming pool and a new indoor swimming baths and theatre were built. With these new facilities, Weston swimming club and water polo team grew into one of the finest in the country. Its most famous member was Paul Radmilovic, winner of several Olympic gold medals between 1904 and 1928.

As with most seaside resorts, many private schools opened throughout the nineteenth and early twentieth centuries, as it became fashionable for the wealthy to send their children to board by the sea. Particular emphasis was placed in the school prospectuses on Weston's healthy air and its benefits for delicate children. The first of these establishments was probably Mr May's boarding school at Moorend Cottage, which opened in the early 1820s. Soon many others were advertising in the papers, including Miss Oliver's School for Young Ladies in South Parade, Mr Pocock's Academy and Miss Sweetapple's Establishment for the Education of Young Ladies. As the century moved on, so several of the larger private mansions were converted into private boarding schools.

Carved stonework on the façade of what is now Ryddenwood Nursing Home, Upper Bristol Road. It marked just one of the many private schools that opened in Weston about the turn of the twentieth century.

The remains of the keel of the Lively, *a collier, driven ashore on Weston beach in a gale in 1886. She was set on fire to mark the Golden Jubilee of Queen Victoria in 1887. These remains were removed in the 1990s as they were believed to be a safety hazard to jet and water skiers.*

The largest of these was The College, a boys' school run by Jonathan Elwell. First opened in Sidmouth House, it moved in 1859 to a purpose-built school on the seafront. This building was sold in the late 1880s and enlarged and converted into the Grand Atlantic Hotel, still in use today. Other private schools included Brynmelyn, Westcliff, Clarence School, Hazelhurst and St Peter's, where the writer Roald Dahl spent four years in the 1920s.

In 1887 celebrations were held in the town to honour the Golden Jubilee of Queen Victoria. The town had always marked big national occasions, from the end of the Peninsular War in 1814 to coronations in 1821 and 1837. In 1814 the celebration consisted of a dinner of roast ox and mutton, laid out on the beach. Everyone attended, from the lowliest villager to the gentry and visitors. After dinner, 'the sprightly dance commenced with true English spirit, without any regard to rank… At night a general illumination took place, in which the Hotel shone most conspicuous'. In 1887 the celebrations were not so different. The streets were decorated and a procession and dinner were followed by a huge fire on Weston beach. Instead of an ordinary bonfire, the wreck of a forty-ton ship, the *Lively*, was loaded with kindling and tar barrels and set alight. The remains of her keel could be seen in the sand beside the Grand Pier until they were finally removed in the 1990s.

Weston became a vital link in national communications when, in 1885, the first of four trans-Atlantic telegraph cables was laid from Weston to Newfoundland, via Waterville in Ireland. Two cottages in Richmond Street were initially taken over as offices but, as demand grew, a purpose-built cable office was built. Further cables were laid in 1901, 1910 and 1923. In 1958 the office became a fully automatic repeater

A carving of a representation of the transatlantic cable, on the façade of the Beach Shelter opposite the Grand Atlantic Hotel.

station until in 1962 telegraphic cables were replaced by the transatlantic telephone and the Richmond Street office was closed. Since then the building has been used as a betting office and night club.

Another new communication link, this time more local, was the building of the Weston, Clevedon and Portishead Light Railway. Although all three towns had a tourism industry to some degree, and rail links in the form of branch lines connecting with the main Bristol and Exeter Railway, there was no direct route between them. An Act of Parliament permitting the line was passed in the 1880s but funding problems meant that it was close on another twenty years before the first train ran, and even then the line terminated at Clevedon. It was another ten years before the final stretch to Portishead was complete. The Weston station was on the corner of Milton and Ashcombe Roads, just up the lane beside the Ashcombe pharmacy which was originally the stationmaster's house. The WC & P as it was known, was always regarded as a comic line. There were many jokes about the slow speed of the trains, such as passengers being able to lean out of the windows and pick blackberries as the train went past, or cowcatchers being needed on the back to stop cows overtaking the train, but its eccentricity endeared it to the public and it became as much a tourist attraction as a useful rail link. It closed in 1940.

The town's boundaries were being pushed ever outwards. In 1902 Milton, originally part of Kewstoke parish, became part of Weston, and much of the southern part of the town, with the Whitecross Estate and surrounding areas, was developed. Unlike the large detached houses on the hillsides, these streets were filled with short terraces or pairs of semi-detached houses with small gardens. These villas did not need huge numbers of servants to run and appealed to middle-income employees and small traders.

Weston ended the nineteenth century with the establishment of an Urban District Council, set up to replace the Town Commissioners and Board of Health. The death of Queen Victoria in 1901 heralded a new age of freedom and changing social customs. The bathing machines were the first to go. In 1903 most of Weston's machines were wrecked in a severe gale and it was unnecessary to replace them. Mixed bathing had finally become socially acceptable when it was tried at Bexhill on Sea two years earlier, and so families could at last bathe together.

Weston-super-Mare is normally renowned for its mild climate and healthy air, indeed one quote has it that 'Weston-super-Mare was made by Weston's Super Air'. However, the weather can turn nasty and some of the greatest local disasters have occurred when high tides and westerly gales coincide. In the Great Gale of 1903, one man drowned whilst trying to fetch help for people stranded in Knightstone Theatre, and tremendous

damage was caused all along the seafront, destroying, among much else, the two jetties on Birnbeck Pier and the slipway at Knightstone. In 1910 water flooded inland up Waterloo Street and the Boulevard as far as Orchard Street, breaking two plate glass shop windows in Lance & Lance's department store on the corner of Waterloo Street and High Street. The newspaper described the sea as 'towering mounds, rising, rocking, falling. Great weird-shaped masses of water dull lead in hue, rose up and disappeared'.

Tourism was a booming industry now. Birnbeck Pier was attracting over 15,000 trippers on a bank holiday, and up to eight steamers could be queuing to disembark their passengers. However, many never made it beyond the pier and traders in the town felt they were losing valuable business. It was hardly surprising, since there was so much on offer on Birnbeck. A contemporary advert lists, among other things, a theatre of wonders, alpine railway, shooting gallery, photographic studios, switchback, waterchute, flying machine, helter skelter, bioscope, cake walk and zigzag slide.

There was another side to the issue in that visitors arriving by rail never made it round the headland to Birnbeck. To resolve both situations, it was decided to build an additional pier, closer to the town centre. And so, in 1904, the first part of the Grand Pier opened, including a pavilion with a 2,000-seat theatre. Here a variety of entertainment was offered. The Carl Rosa and D'Oyly Carte opera companies regularly performed and such stars of the day as Dame Clara Butt, George Robey, Vesta Tilley and Ralph Richardson all appeared there. As well as the theatre, there was an outdoor bandstand where Italian, German and Viennese bands played

The remains of Weston's bathing machines on the promenade after the Great Gale of September 1903.

Birnbeck Pier in its heyday. The lifeboat house is on the left.

Grand Pier Pavilion and bandstand, c. 1905.

This promotional postcard issued by the Great Western Railway shows a general view over Weston Bay. The Grand Pier is being extended to enable paddle steamers to berth. This was not successful and the extra length was removed in 1916.

daily concerts and special times were set aside to allow devotees of the new craze of roller skating to glide up and down the pier.

Because of the gently sloping beach, steamers were still restricted to using Birnbeck. However, in an attempt to allow boats to berth at the Grand Pier, a further length of 450m was built out to deeper water. The treacherous currents proved too much though and, after a few attempts, the steamer companies decided it was too dangerous. The extra length of pier was dismantled in 1916 aside from a short section beyond the pavilion.

Electricity was the new clean power of the future and in 1901 a power station was built in Locking Road. An electricity supply allowed the building of a tramway system, officially opened the following year. On Whit Monday 1902, over 12,500 passengers were carried, although one wit remarked that the electric cables, carried on cast iron brackets, made Weston Sea Front look like an 'elongated clothes-line'! There was no set timetable as the trams ran according to demand. If a steamer was due at the pier there might be seven or eight cars waiting to carry the passengers into town; if the weather was fine the open cross-bench cars would be brought out, returning to the depot if the weather changed for the worse. The trams were not universally popular as they took business away from the horse-drawn cabs and wagonettes. The drivers began a policy of obstruction, parking vehicles across tracks or driving slowly in front of the trams. This grew to such an extent that it had to be stopped by court order.

However, the trams in their turn had to deal with similar competition. As early as 1903 a Daimler motor wagonette was operating from Birnbeck Pier to Marine Parade. Later, motor buses would sometimes race the trams to get to passengers first, often resulting in a derailment, or in the tram's trolley boom becoming de-wired on corners. In 1937 the battle was lost and the tramway closed for the last time. Until recent years the tram shed

Trams and wagonettes waiting for passengers from the steamer at Birnbeck Pier, c. 1910.

was still in use, as Cashman's DIY store, but the site has recently been developed with housing.

Weston has been home to many famous people over the years. In 1912 the novelist Mary Webb moved to the town with her new husband, Henry. It was whilst here that she wrote *The Golden Arrow*, together with two poems, although her most famous novel is *Precious Bane*. Other writers with local connections include Roald Dahl who went to school at St Peters and Jeffrey Archer, later Lord Archer of Weston-super-Mare and Mark, who was born in the town and lived here until his teens. Other Westonians include actors John Cleese and Rupert Graves, both of whom were born in the town.

Nor did Weston escape its part in major world events. The same year that Mary Webb arrived, RMS *Titanic* sank in the Atlantic. A Weston family, Mr Louch, Sunday school superintendent and deacon at Clarence Park Baptist Church, and his wife were on board on their way to California. Mrs Louch made it to a lifeboat but her husband drowned.

Greater disaster soon loomed however, with the outbreak of the First World War.

CHAPTER 7
The First World War and Post-war Frivolity

In the autumn of 1914 the outbreak of war overshadowed everything. The first tangible evidence locally of the terror starting in Flanders was the arrival of Belgian refugees. The first group of sixteen men, women and children arrived in November 1914 and lodged at Clifford House in Walliscote Road. More soon followed until by March the following year there were nearly 100 in Weston alone, with others in nearby villages. Some died here, mainly as a result of the suffering they had endured before fleeing Belgium, and in 1922 a stone of Cornish granite was set up in Weston cemetery to commemorate them. The survivors were gradually able to return, until by 1917 all had gone home.

As the death toll grew on the battlefronts, increasing numbers of soldiers were needed. In the drive to encourage men to volunteer, one man with Weston roots produced a work of art still recognized today. Artist Alfred Leete produced many cartoons, satirical drawings and advertisements, but his striking poster of Lord Kitchener pointing his finger with the words 'Your Country Needs You' has to be his most well-known work. In 1893 Leete moved to Weston with his parents, where they ran two hotels, Sutherland House and Addington House. He was apprenticed to a Bristol architect, before turning to art as a career. Despite a lifetime spent mainly in London, he never forgot his home town and it is in Weston cemetery that he now lies, his gravestone bearing a bronze plaque with his distinctive signature.

Many recruits were billeted in Weston as they underwent basic training before being posted abroad. The beach was ideal for practicing digging trenches and rifle-butts were set up at Sand Bay for target practice. Westonians were quick to rally round and offer support to these new visitors. Clarence Park Baptist church opened up its school room as somewhere the soldiers could go and relax. There, newspapers were provided, as well as materials to write letters home. In 1915 the parishioners also set up a Comforts Fund, sending letters, cigarettes and chocolate to men at the battle fronts.

The timber in Weston Woods was a valuable war resource and over eighty per cent of the trees were felled, dragged down from the woods by horses, loaded onto trolleys and taken along the Toll Road to the railway yards for transportation. The wood was used for a variety of military

Memorial stone for the Belgian refugees who died in Weston during the First World War.

*Some of the patients
and staff at Ashcombe
House Red Cross
Hospital during the
First World War.*

*Opposite: War Memorial
in Grove Park. The
column surmounted by a
bronze casting of winged
Victory was designed by
Alfred Drury and
installed in 1922. 380
names are inscribed on
the bronze panels.*

purposes. Ash was used in the new aircraft industry, whilst other timber was used for tent pegs, firewood and for shoring trenches. At home some went to provide pit props in the mines. As well as losing woodland, green spaces were ploughed for food production, including the meadow in front of Glebe House and the Hotel Field, now the site of the Winter Gardens.

Ashcombe House, once the mansion of the Capell family, was commandeered for use by the Red Cross as a hospital for wounded soldiers, and local girls worked as Voluntary Aid Detachment nurses there. The transatlantic cables and the office in Richmond Street were vital communication links and guards were posted to protect them at all times. Also placed under guard was the Electric Generating Station in Locking Road. In 1916 the Managing Engineer's proposal to engage women as tram drivers was approved and Weston had the distinction of having the first female tram drivers in the West Country.

The whole local fleet of paddle-steamers was requisitioned during the war, although a skeleton service across to Wales was maintained with chartered boats. After the war only nine out of the fourteen ships were returned for use, the others lost by enemy action or overuse.

In 1922, at a solemn ceremony in Grove Park, a memorial was unveiled to the 380 men of Weston, Uphill, and Kewstoke, killed during the war. Now the time had come to move forward. The end of the war led to an initial period of prosperity and a national need for fun and pleasure. A new wave of building took place over the next few years. Following

Addison's Act of 1919, Milton Green was the site for the first council housing in Britain. Other housing followed, including Milton Brow and the second phase of the Bournville Estate. In addition the interwar years gave us some of the town's most well-known landmarks, notably, the Marine Lake, Open Air Pool, airport, Odeon cinema and the Winter Gardens and Pavilion.

The idea of a Winter Gardens for the town dates back to the 1880s when the subject was first discussed as 'a means of postponing the autumn and of mitigating the region of winter; a place affording shade, shelter, rest and recreation to some, while it will afford accommodation for fêtes, balls, concerts, lectures, croquet, lawn tennis and every description of out-of-doors amusements, not for summer or winter only, but for all year round'. Two sites were then considered. The first, Rogers' Field next to the Royal Hotel, was thought the best option but the hotel had restrictive covenants on the site to protect its views, so the other option of a site in the Boulevard was chosen. The Summer and Winter Gardens were duly opened in August 1882. This building underwent several changes of use over its lifetime, including concert hall, roller-skating rink, theatre and cinema until its destruction during the Second World War. The site is now occupied by Tivoli House flats.

The town still needed a larger public ballroom, to replace the old Assembly Rooms in West Street. These had been built in 1859 with shops on the ground floor and a large room on the first floor, used for concerts, dances and public meetings. However, the room was too small to cater for the huge increase in population and visitor numbers, so in 1922 the council revived its original plan and bought Rogers' Field.

The Italian Gardens fronting the High Street were finished first. It had been planned to use a hedge to separate them from the putting green behind but, Harry Brown, the Town Surveyor, discovered a stone terrace with statuary and seating for sale amongst old aeroplane parts at Beddington House, Croydon. The 61m-long terrace was perfect to face the High Street and the plans were adjusted to make space for it. Unfortunately vandalism in recent years has decimated this terrace and only four of the original nine statues remain.

In August 1925 the putting green, Rose Garden, Lily Pond and the Alpine Garden were opened to the public. The eighteen-hole putting green was turfed with grass from the original Rogers' Field as it was already sea-washed and hardy to the salt air. This last tenuous link with old Weston was finally lost when the site was redeveloped in 1990. In 1927 the Pavilion was officially opened by Sir Ernest Palmer, deputy chairman of the Great Western Railway. Inside, the ballroom floor was sunk to below ground level, a unique way of overcoming the covenants restricting the height of the building. In 1990 the pavilion underwent a major

One of the four remaining sculptures on the Portland stone terrace at the Italian Gardens. They represented the four seasons, together with reaping, sowing, humility, childhood and vanity.

refurbishment and a large conference complex was built to the rear so that today, the Winter Gardens still provide Weston's main public space as dances, conferences and antique fairs continue to draw residents and tourists alike all year round.

The same year that the Winter Gardens opened, work began on constructing the Marine Lake by building a causeway across Glentworth Bay. The aim was to create a part of the beach where the tide was always in and which could then be used for boating, swimming and other marine activities. People still flocked to the seaside to enjoy bathing and another major scheme to be completed between the wars was the Open Air Pool, in 1937. As well as a large swimming pool, it offered a café and platforms for the new activity of sunbathing. Its most striking feature was the Art Deco-style concrete diving boards, which at one time were used for elaborate synchronised diving displays. The boards were demolished in the early 1980s when the pool was remodelled as the Tropicana. Today the building is closed awaiting redevelopment. The proposed scheme suggests a much larger building, housing a splash pool, cinema, health suites and restaurant and would involve the demolition of the existing building and the excavation of the Beach Lawns for underground car parking. It seems likely that the council will pass the plans and the Tropicana 2 could be open by 2004.

The early years of the twentieth century saw the birth of the film industry and people began to flock see the new movies. 'Electric Moving Pictures'

The Open Air Pool, shortly after its opening in 1937.

The Odeon cinema was designed by T. Cecil Howitt in the Art Deco style, and opened in 1935. Today it is the only remaining Howitt cinema still screening films.

were first shown in Weston in 1911 at Knightstone Theatre as short highlights between the shows. That same year the Electric cinema opened on the site now occupied by the Odeon cinema. Within a month of it opening it was showing a film of B.C. Hucks, the first man to fly the Bristol Channel. Two years later the Regent Picture House opened in Regent Street. Later renamed the Gaumont, it became a bingo hall in 1973 and was finally demolished in the 1980s. Films became so popular that three more cinemas opened. In 1921 the Central cinema opened in Oxford Street. Seating 650 people, it was the first cinema in Weston to have the full equipment to show talkies. The Palace Theatre was converted to show films and was renamed the Tivoli cinema and finally, in 1935, the old Electric cinema was replaced by the Odeon. This superb building was designed by T. Cecil Howitt in the Art Deco style and was listed in 1986 as being of outstanding historical interest. Many changes to the building have taken place over the years and the cinema now boasts four screens, but the original Compton theatre organ is still played regularly.

One of the most spectacular events in Weston's history occurred on the night of 13 January 1930, when the Grand Pier Pavilion caught fire. Gale force winds fanned the flames and sparks were showered on houses as far away as South Road. To the pier's misfortune, the water main that supplied the hydrants had been turned off as a precaution against frost. By the time the fire was finally doused, the Edwardian theatre had been totally destroyed. It was three years before a new pavilion was built as some shareholders suggested it be resited at the shore end. However, the council refused and it was rebuilt as before. Instead of housing a theatre though, it contained amusement machines and rides which were then more profitable. Today it is the largest pavilion on any pier and still hosts a funfair and arcade games.

Gradually the horse-drawn wagonettes and brakes gave way to motor charabancs and coaches. Weston Tramway closed as motor buses offered greater flexibility over routes. Trains were still the most popular and convenient way to travel any distance and to resolve the situation of excursion trains blocking the main platforms, a separate excursion station had been built in 1914. This was situated beside the goods station on Locking Road where Hildesheim Court and Tesco stand today. One always knew when a train had arrived as crowds would be seen making their way up Regent Street to the beach.

In the 1930s the biggest change in transport was the arrival of air travel. Before the First World War, small aeroplanes began offering short joyrides to passengers, taking off and landing on the beach or in a field in Locking Road. In 1936, Weston airfield was built. Here, Western

Motor cars and charabancs line the promenade in this picture taken in the late 1930s. The ornate iron posts once carried the electric cables for the tramway which closed in 1937.

One of the biplanes that offered joy rides to tourists from the beach at Uphill, c. 1912.

Airways operated scheduled air taxi services to many parts of the country. These became so popular that after the first weekend of operation the *Weston Mercury* reported that 'flights were so overbooked that additional air liners had to be brought into use'. Particularly popular was the ten-minute cross-channel service to Wales. Both Weston and Cardiff airports were close to their respective town centres and many South Wales miners flew over to enjoy the delights of Weston on their days off. It should be remembered that Wales was 'dry' on Sundays, and airport staff were warned to look out for those who had been indulging in Weston's pubs a little too freely! Over the 1937 Whitsun holiday, over 2500 passengers travelled on Western Airways from the Airport, a world record for that time.

After the First World War, a large military tank had been placed in Alexandra Parade to commemorate local efforts on behalf of War Savings. By the 1930s this was a dilapidated and rusty relic and people were tired of this constant reminder of the war. With thousands of excursionists arriving at Locking Road station opposite, it was felt an attractive new feature was needed. The Parks Superintendent, Percy Norman, came up with the idea of a Floral Clock. It was not the first floral clock in Weston. There have been ornamental flower beds in Weston's parks since the nineteenth century, using the Victorian technique of carpet bedding to create a picture out of flowers and foliage plants. In both Clarence and Grove Parks, beds were laid out as flower clocks, but these had wooden hands for show only. The Alexandra Parade clock would actually work. The semi-circular face was made of built-up soil held by a stone retaining wall. The hands were hollow metal troughs and were also planted with flowers. The feature became hugely popular with visitors. As part of the Festival of Britain celebrations in 1951, it was decided to revamp the clock. The old planted hands were changed for lighter plain wooden ones and a cuckoo

The Floral Clock, planted for the centenary of the NSPCC in 1984.

was installed to mark the hours and half-hours. The *Municipal Journal* reported that:

> An electronic cuckoo is one of the new features of the reconstructed floral clock at Weston-super-Mare... The cuckoo is housed in a timber chalet... The bird is housed in the top half of the chalet and the naval type of loudspeaker is housed in the lower part behind the metal grille. The bird, which is made of teak, is an exact reproduction of the cuckoo but enlarged with a length of 15 inches. At the hour and half-hour the bird emerges from the chalet and the two notes are sounded, one for the half-hour and one for each hour recorded by the clock hand.

This bird not only glided out of its chalet and cuckooed but dipped and flapped its wings and was soon attracting crowds of holidaymakers every time it was due to appear. The clock is still a feature today, although the hands and cuckoo have long-since been abandoned, due to constant vandalism.

The inter-war years culminated in the town being granted Borough status in 1937. Councillor Henry Butt was rewarded for all his efforts on behalf of the town and became the first mayor while 'Ever Forward' was chosen for the town's motto on the coat of arms.

Weston Borough Council coat of arms, 1937.

CHAPTER 8
The Second World War

On 1 September 1939, German soldiers invaded Poland and Prime Minister Neville Chamberlain announced, 'this country is now at war with Germany'. War had been expected and some precautions had already been taken. Gas masks and materials for air-raid shelters had been distributed and everyone one had been issued with an identity card.

It was believed that, if war broke out, one third of the entire population would be under threat of air raids and so a large-scale evacuation plan had been prepared. As soon as war was declared, children most at risk in the larger cities were moved to rural areas such as the West Country. Weston-super-Mare was one of the evacuation centres and the first group soon arrived. However, rather than the expected arrival of city children, the first evacuees were almost 400 American citizens sent on the advice of the American Consul in Bristol. A London newspaper reported that 'Evacuees will camp in the amusement park (Grand Pier), where army huts are being erected, with camp beds among their equipment...' In reality most of these evacuees sought somewhere a little more comfortable, such as local hotels, notably the Grand Atlantic.

Soon afterwards the first British evacuees arrived – over 10,000 children and pregnant women from the East End of London. On arrival at Locking Road excursion station the children were sent to general accommodation depots, such as at Walliscote School and Milton Road Infants' School where they were given a drink and a bun, and a 24-hour ration pack. Just over half stayed in Weston, whilst the rest were sent out to the neighbouring villages.

The extra numbers of residents, albeit temporary, required a great deal of administration and various committees were set up to deal with any problems. One issue concerned the weekly Government payment of 8s 6d given to those who agreed to look after an evacuee. Hosts complained that the sea air stimulated the appetites of the children, so increasing the amount of food they ate! A small rise in the payment was eventually agreed. The Borough Council set up a communal laundry at Knightstone Baths and a Welfare Committee organised an additional maternity home at Allandale on Beach Road. Even in times like these, children had to continue their education and local schools set up shift systems to cope with the increased numbers. About 130 evacuees spent the whole of the war in the town and a few made Weston their permanent home. Most returned after a few months however, as homesickness overcame their fear of air raids.

The first bombs fell on Weston on 14 August 1940. These exploded beside the Open Air Pool and an air-raid warden was reported to have been 'splattered with good honest Weston mud as far away as Whitecross Road'. There were other occasional raids that year, including one which destroyed the boating pool in Ashcombe Park, but it was in January 1941 and June 1942 that the town suffered most. During these overnight raids large areas of the town were destroyed and some of its most well-known landmarks lost, including the Tivoli Cinema, Boulevard Congregational church, Grove Park Pavilion and Lance & Lance's department store on the corner of Waterloo Street and High Street. Other damage occurred in Oxford Street, Orchard Street, Wadham Street, and Prospect Place as well as residential areas further from the centre.

In the nine-hour raid on the night of 4 January 1941, eighty-five people were injured and thirty four killed, among them evacuee children from London and the well-known local one-armed footballer, Frank Addicott. Bob Payne, the caretaker of Bournville School, won the BEM for tunnelling through debris to rescue eight survivors. Three thousand incendiaries and thirty high explosive bombs fell on Weston that night.

The heaviest raids, however, came on two successive nights in June 1942, when 102 people were killed and over 400 injured. Almost 100 high explosive bombs and 10,000 incendiary bombs fell on the resort. A

Allandale, Beach Road, Weston. This was opened as an additional maternity home to cater for the influx of evacuees during the Second World War.

Lance and Lance's department store from a letterhead of about 1920.

graphic account survives in the Log Book of St Margaret's Home for Children in Queens Road, Weston, kept by the matron, Miss Pike:

Sunday June 28th
A night of horror! An unexpected and very sudden air raid. The enemy planes were swooping right down over us – the back of our house was lit up – we could see it thro' the black-out… Incendiary bombs fell all around us – the house opposite – Mr & Mrs Barclay, Woodford, All Saints Road, was in flames. They and their maid and two evacuee girls they had since the beginning of the war, all came to our shelter… Margaret and I made tea for our guests and for Wardens etc. hard at work outside. There were fires all around us. All the children and staff are safe.

Monday June 29th
Another night of 'Hell on Earth'. The siren went about the same time and before I had the children down, the sparks from enemy machine gun fire were coming into our green dormitory where the windows had been blasted Saturday night. We were on our way downstairs when there was a terrific bang. It must have been the H.E. dropped in Grove Park Road… Last night the raid in some respects was worse than Saturday night. After the 'All Clear' when I went round the house – the whole town looked to be ablaze…

No bread came this morning and… I heard our baker's had been destroyed, I went down to the Food Office this afternoon. The town is terrible. I had to go a long way round as streets and roads are guarded – unexploded bombs and buildings in a dangerous state… After seeing what I have I shall not send the children to school this week or allow them to see any of the damage until the town has been cleared up a little. It is not a fit sight for any child to see needlessly nor is it safe.

Some of the raiding aircraft dived so low that they were seen to take violent avoiding action to clear high buildings, and one actually flew along the Boulevard level with the first floor windows. Although the centre of town got hit the hardest, there were also many incidents further out.

There were several reasons for Weston being deliberately targeted. This area had vital communication lines, not least the terminus for the transatlantic cable in Richmond Street. There were also the aircraft factories that surrounded the town. In the early 1940s the Bristol Aeroplane Company were producing Avro Anson aeroplanes at Weston. Other production took place at the Elborough factory near Locking, which was built during the war for the fabrication of parts for the new Beaufighter aircraft which was then assembled at Oldmixon. Another reason for the raids is thought to have been a report in a local newspaper. It showed people enjoying themselves on the sands and had the caption 'Weston doesn't know there's a war on!' After the raid Lord Haw Haw was heard on the radio saying that perhaps Weston did now know there was a war on. The last bombs fell in March 1944 when incendiaries were dropped on the Bournville Estate.

Charged with the task of spotting approaching enemy aircraft were the men and women of the Royal Observer Corps. There were several posts in the Weston area, including one in the ruined windmill on Uphill Hill. Another defence against aircraft were barrage balloons. These static hydrogen-filled balloons were moored above vulnerable buildings to put attacking aircraft off course. To meet the demand for fuel for the balloons deployed in the western barrages, ICI set up a new hydrogen production plant at Weston.

A number of anti-aircraft sites were established around the town and the immediate area, including at the BAC Oldmixon factory, Hutton, Uphill and Worlebury. These were part of the perimeter defences for Bristol, but also served to protect Weston. Another local defence was a decoy set up on Bleadon Hill. This was a series of lights and earthworks, laid out to mimic a town seen at night. This proved its worth on several occasions, diverting bombers on night attacks on Weston.

In 1941, Birnbeck Pier was commandeered by the Royal Navy. Commander Charles Goodeve RNVR was first Deputy Director of the Department of Miscellaneous Weapons Development and was searching for a suitable place to carry out secret weapons testing and research. Although the main base was at Birnbeck, testing also took place in Sand Bay and at Brean Down, where the high tidal range allowed weapons to be exploded under water and retrieved at low tide for inspection. There was also close liaison with RAF Locking where a trials aircraft was based. The author Nevil Shute was stationed on

Veterans of HMS Birnbeck, visiting the pier in 1998. From left, Louis Klemetaski, Duncan Bruce and James Close.

HMS *Birnbeck* for a short period. The weapons worked on were both offensive and defensive, and included hedgehog and squid mines, the quick-shooting star shell, midget submarines, special gear to help climb the cliffs at Arromanches in Normandy and rockets that threw out a chain mat to deter low-flying aircraft. Unconfirmed reports also say that some of the development of the Mulberry Harbour and PLUTO (pipeline under the ocean) took place there. It was not unusual for the odd rocket to go astray and many a greenhouse was hit on occasion.

As well as the Navy, there were also RAF troops in Weston for training and a number of complaints were made about the bad language sometimes used by the airmen as they drilled on the seafront, especially by mothers with children!

With the need to conserve resources and recycle materials, there were big changes in everyday life. Every available area was turned over to food production, including parks, gardens and, in some cases grass verges. A WVS Clothing Exchange was set up in the Swan Hotel in Regent Street and people were encouraged to salvage and recycle anything suitable. Metal was particularly important and many buildings lost their iron railings at this time, as can be seen by the rows of sawn-off stumps along the top of many garden walls. Only where a safety hazard would be created were people allowed to keep them. Disused railway lines were another source of scrap metal and the by now defunct Weston, Clevedon & Portishead Light Railway was estimated to contain sufficient steel to construct at least 100 Churchill tanks. When it was learned that the rails were made in Berlin there was considerable satisfaction in sending it back to Germany in the form of bombs. In fact, the metal salvaged was rarely of much use and it was more important as a morale booster than for any practical purpose.

Even the famous floral clock was put to use and was planted with the slogan 'Lend to Defend – National War Savings'. The Government was in desperate need of money as the cost of the war grew. By 1940, munitions were costing up to £7 million a day. National Savings were established and campaigns run for special causes such as 'Salute the Soldier', 'Warship Week' and 'Wings for Victory'. Towns that raised a sufficient amount in War Savings were allowed to adopt ships and planes. Weston-super-Mare raised almost £400,000 to adopt HMS *Weston*. HMS *Weston-super-Mare* was a Falmouth-class escort sloop launched in July 1932. She was named in honour of Lord Alexander, a politician and First Lord of the Admiralty during the war, who was born in George Street, Weston-super-Mare in 1883. Sailors soon nicknamed her 'Aggie-on-horseback' after Dame Agnes Weston, founder of the Sailor's Homes, after which the Navy shortened her name to H.M.S. *Weston*. After a distinguished war service the ship was scrapped in 1947. Another successful campaign was the 'Spitfire for Weston' Fund.

Trains still ran where possible although several bombs were dropped onto the railway lines damaging five out of the six road bridges crossing the tracks. People were discouraged from anything but essential travel, however. Entertainment was still available and indeed was vital to keep up morale. Knightstone Theatre was closed for the duration whilst it was used as a factory producing army uniforms but other venues still functioned. The BBC used the Winter Gardens to broadcast several radio programmes until the first of the major air raids, after which they decided

Stubs in this wall at Church Road Methodist church show where cast iron railings were removed for salvage during the Second World War.

The Floral Clock, planted with the slogan 'Lend to Defend', to encourage people to invest in National Savings.

*Advertisement in the
Weston Gazette in aid of
the Weston-super-Mare
Warship Week appeal.*

North Wales was probably safer and moved to Bangor.

By late 1943 a build-up of troops and equipment began throughout the whole of the south of England ready for D-Day. The first troops to arrive in Weston were the Green Howards, who camped in the woods. They were soon followed by American soldiers, including the 116th Anti-Aircraft Gun Battalion (Mobile) of the Coast Artillery Corps – B Battery – with the First US Army, the 109th AAA Gun Battalion, HHB 11th AAA Group, 531st AAA Automatic Weapons Battalion and the 16th Ordnance Bomb Disposal Squad.

The majority of the soldiers were billeted in local hotels and boarding houses, requisitioned for the purpose. These included The Rozel, the Grand Atlantic, Hotel Villa Rosa and The Cairo Hotel. Others soldiers were placed with local residents or in a large tented encampment on the Beach Lawns. Part of Weston Golf Course was occupied by soldiers from a US mobile gun battery. Black and white troops were strictly segregated at that time and people remember fights breaking out between the soldiers, especially outside the Queens Hotel in Regent Street, a favourite drinking place.

However, most local people welcomed the visitors, and took the soldiers into their hearts and homes. Many long-standing friendships were formed. Great efforts were made to entertain the troops and in return the

*American GIs outside
their billet at 115 Severn
Road, Weston.*

Americans were generous guests, giving away food, chocolate, nylon stockings and other items not seen in Britain for many years. The newspapers reported the weddings of several 'GI brides', local girls who married American soldiers. As one M. Ventola said

> This was our kind of town. We met Lina and her mother and father, who fled Mussolini's Italy to open an Italian-style sweet shop and ice cream parlour. Between our goodies from home, canned tomatoes, sugar and some goodies Sgt Woyjeck gave us, we found a home away from home. At Lina's we had home-made spaghetti, ice cream etc. Wow, what a treat for us!

Michael Kruglinksi, Captain CAC, Battery Commander, also had fond memories of his time at Weston-super-Mare:

> Looking at the swimming pool, we were a few blocks to the left. At first our Battery headquarters was in a small corner hotel (fanciest in the area) with sandstone detail… While we were in Wales for target shooting a higher headquarters took it from us. As I returned around March 1, I went to inspect some civilian billets assigned to some of our displaced men. In one case I found the lady stuffing hot water bottles in the bed for the comfort of new arrivals.

The GIs spent their time training and preparing their equipment, often travelling to Wales or the Devon coast. As part of their training at least one locally-stationed battalion took part in Operation Tiger at Slapton Sands in Devon. This event became notorious as a German E-boat surprised the troops and many were killed.

In addition to troops, large quantities of military vehicles were stockpiled in the town. Vehicles belonging to the 116th Anti-Aircraft Battalion were parked in Weston Woods on both sides of Worlebury Hill Road, protected by a machine gun at each end of the column. During the day, personnel worked on the vehicles, preparing them for the Channel crossing to France. At night they returned to camps and billets leaving only sentries on guard duty. Many of these guards were young city boys and were terrified of the pitch-black woodland with its ancient hillfort and strange animal noises!

As D-Day approached, General Eisenhower visited the troops at Weston, on his morale-boosting tour through the South of England. He stayed the night in a caravan in Weston Woods beside the Water Tower. Slowly, a mighty armada of troopships assembled in the Bristol Channel stretching from Portishead to Lundy Island. One night people heard what they thought was the sound of thunder, but in the morning all the soldiers and ships had gone. Several days later the local beaches were littered with American food packaging from the emergency rations on which the troops had been fed.

Weston's part in D-Day did not end when the soldiers left. Five thousand units of blood were donated by Weston people and the *Weston-super-Mare Gazette* of 17 June 1944 reported that 'Within an hour of the landings in Normandy, blood transfusions were being given to the wounded on the beaches. The blood of the people of Weston-super-Mare is now on the beaches of France'.

The GIs left behind a permanent reminder of their stay here. An American plant, a horsetail, was found in Ellenborough Park where American troops had been camped. It is believed that the seed must have been brought to Weston in a GI's trouser turn-up! The only other occurrence of this particular horsetail in Britain is in Lincoln, on a wartime US airbase.

On 8 May 1945 the celebrations for VE Day began. The mayor made a speech from the steps of the town hall and soon the streets were packed with thousands of people. A short Thanksgiving service followed the mayor's speech and then for one day people went wild. Fireworks could be heard all over Weston and pianos and other musical instruments were brought out on to the streets so that there could be singing and dancing. Pubs were allowed to stay open until midnight and impromptu dances were held, including at the Rozel Bandstand, the promenade opposite the Swimming Pool and at the Winter Gardens Pavilion where band music was relayed to the crowd outside. As night fell the Victory lights went on and for the first time since the war began, cinemas, the town hall, Winter Gardens, Knightstone and Victoria Methodist church were floodlit. Bonfires were lit on the beach and after so many years of blackout the town came alive.

Reality soon set in, however. People were exhausted after five long years of war. The town was scarred with numerous bomb sites, housing was in short supply, and transport needs had to be addressed. The time had come to rebuild for the future.

CHAPTER 9

Post-war Decline and Regeneration

The Second World War gave people new ideas and values, and the post-war period became one of rebirth and renewal as the country moved from a time of austerity and rationing to embrace a new philosophy of mass consumerism.

The Government first set about lifting the remaining wartime restrictions and controls and increasing exports. Reminders of the war were still part of everyday life long after peace was declared. Soap was rationed until 1950, and some foods were still on ration as late as 1954.

In 1951 the Festival of Britain was held, to encourage the nation towards building a future and to advertise the country's achievements and stimulate industry. The opening of the festival was officially marked in Weston by a service at the Beach Lawns Bandstand. There then followed a variety of events throughout the year. In May the most prestigious occasion was a performance of Bach's *St Matthew Passion* at the Victoria Methodist Church and the Parish Church by the 1951 Festival Choir of 100 voices. A special town guide was launched, although only 40,000 copies were able to be printed as there was still a paper shortage, and other events included beauty pageants, cake competitions, exhibitions and flower festivals.

It was during this period that 'youth culture' was born. The word 'teenager' was first used in the 1950s and young people had money of their own to spend due to full employment and increased wages. Rock and roll, coffee bars and young fashion emerged. These changes affected seaside resorts too. As young people developed their own identity so the teddy boy, and later mod and rocker, movements formed, leading to well-publicized battles in some coastal towns in the 1960s.

In common with many other towns in the country, Weston had to rethink its direction and plan for the future. No longer could British seaside resorts rely on families booking their annual week by the sea, when increasing disposable income and developments in air transport were making foreign resorts accessible. Bomb sites still punctuated Weston's streets and this, combined with a general feeling of wanting to wipe away the past and look to the future, led towards large-scale redevelopment plans being drafted.

In 1947 a report was drawn up by Lionel Brett and Clough Williams-

Laura Buildings, one of many small courts and lanes built in the 1840s and demolished just over 100 years later for redevelopment. In the background is the tower of Emmanuel church.

Ellis (the architect famous for Portmeirion village in Wales) on the suggested post-war redevelopment of Weston. They proposed wide-scale demolition and rebuilding to a new town plan. 'What remains of old Weston is so fragmentary that it must be written off where it conflicts with the general reconstruction scheme.' The newspapers reported heated debates over whether to reconstruct or redevelop bombed areas. All this was brought to a head over the 'Battle of Waterloo Street'. This part of the town had probably suffered in the war more than any other in Weston. Lance & Lance's store on the south-east corner of High Street had been destroyed as well as buildings on the north-east corner of Waterloo Street and High Street and the Boulevard Congregational church on the corner of Longton Grove Road. It was suggested that an eighty-foot dual-carriageway replace Waterloo Street, by taking the Boulevard north along Worthy Place and meeting the seafront at West Street in a straight line, sweeping away all in its path. Needless to say it didn't happen!

Instead, Weston Borough Council wanted to make improvements by redeveloping a large area in the centre of the town. This in its turn caused another major controversy as it involved the demolition of some 120 homes. The council put compulsory purchase orders on properties in Carlton Street, Little Carlton Street, Castle Street, New Street, Sidmouth Cottages East and West, Maine Square, Atlantic Cottages and Shaddick's Cottages – all forming a tight-knit community of early nineteenth-century courts and lanes centred around Carlton Street.

The dispute dragged on for years. In August 1957 a group was set up by the residents of the affected area. Known as the League of Home Defence, their aim was to fight against the clearance orders and bring as much publicity to the issue as possible. The editorial in the *Weston Mercury* in November 1957 wrote, 'Weston's motto may be "Ever Forward", but that does not give us the undisputed right to push ahead in a reckless "damn the consequences" attitude'.

There were two main causes of upset. Firstly the dispersal of the community and secondly the fact that the houses had been declared 'unfit for human habitation'. Most of the residents were aged between fifty-two and eighty-nine and, in some cases, had lived there all their lives. They were understandably upset at having their homes called slums. They were also unhappy at being offered council houses at Earlham Grove, Milton and Oldmixon, as they were all some distance from the town centre and some way from each other. A public enquiry was held as fifty-six objectors registered their opposition to the plan. A year later a decision by the Minister of Housing gave temporary reprieve to fifty properties. Demolition began on the remainder.

In 1961, Chamberlain, Powell & Bon were appointed to prepare designs for the redevelopment of this area. Their brief was to cater for the town's continuing expansion of population, light industry and future tourism needs. Their proposal included a hotel, conference centre, new library, cinema, flats, shopping arcade, town hall extension and car parking. In the event, financial backing could not be obtained for the scheme and it was abandoned. The site was subsequently developed to form the Dolphin Square shopping precinct with the remainder left as the Carlton Street Car Park. At the back of the car park you can still see the remains of fireplaces and doorways of the old cottages that were torn down. Dolphin Square never achieved its aim of encouraging shoppers to the southern end of the High Street and today it is very much a secondary shopping centre although the recent traffic schemes and pedestrianization in High Street South may help to remedy this.

The Carlton Street site was not the only part of the town scheduled for clearance. Union Street had already been flattened and widened with

The sad remnants of demolished houses in the back wall of the Carlton Street car park. These fireplaces and fragmentary walls are all that remain of Maine Square and Sidmouth Cottages.

Dolphin Square Shopping Centre, 2002. Originally a fibreglass dolphin sculpture ornamented this square. The children's play area and umbrellas were added in 1999.

new Government offices built on the eastern side. Plans for this area included new shops and a multi-storey car park and required the demolition of Laura Buildings, Wilcox Place, Regent Place and parts of Regent Street, one scheme which did go ahead as planned.

Despite the huge areas of damage and renewal, other parts of the town were still virtually unaltered from the early twentieth century. Small independent specialist shops still formed the bulk of the retail areas. Self-service supermarkets did not open in Weston until the late 1950s and the large multiples had not yet turned the High Street into a carbon copy of every other high street in the country.

Another major national effort was concentrated on relieving the housing shortage as local authorities were given a national target of building 300,000 homes a year. Housing and car parking were deemed to be the main priorities as the population was growing as rapidly as car ownership. In 1931 the census recorded Weston's population as just over 28,000; by 1951 it was over 40,000. The Oldmixon and Coronation Estates were both built in the 1950s and early 1960s, growing from small numbers of prefabs to the mixture of flats, houses, schools and shops there today. In addition the Bournville Estate was extended. While their borders meet, and despite similar social problems, each estate has retained its separate identity and community spirit to this day.

The car parking problem was harder to resolve. As wages rose and car prices fell, car ownership grew dramatically. Before the war there was no permanent off-road car parking in Weston besides the Melrose Car Park, which was mostly used for coaches. After the war some cleared bomb sites provided approximately 390 spaces. Conservative estimates of future needs were 1000 spaces – many of these to be generated by the Carlton Street scheme, the new multi-storey planned for Union Street and the proposed demolition of Palmer Street for another multi-storey car park, fortunately abandoned.

The war had brought much new industry to Weston. Afterwards, many of the firms remained in the town, switching over to making peacetime products, while others left vacant factory premises. One example was the Bristol Aeroplane Company. When the war ended, the factory transferred to making prefabricated aluminium bungalows to combat the initial housing shortage. Later they also started to make larger buildings such as schools and hospitals, which were exported to countries as far away as Australia. They then went on to make parts for civil aircraft such as the Bristol Britannia for BOAC. In 1954 they converted production to helicopters, being taken over by Westlands six years later. Westlands remained one of the town's major employers until it announced the closure of the Weston works in 2002.

In 1958 the Borough Council began to actively promote Weston as a base for light industry in order to provide a broader range of employment opportunities. The Town Development Act of 1952 had been passed to facilitate the movement of people and industry from overpopulated parts of the country. Under the Act Weston used its long association with the Midlands to encourage firms to move to Weston. The council sold or leased sites and buildings along Winterstoke Road and council housing was made available for those workers wishing to move here. One result was that Clarks Shoes opened its Bushacre factory in Locking Road. Clarks was another of the town's major employers that has recently closed its Weston factory.

Despite these stories of disputes and huge building projects, residents and tourists were well-catered for during this period. Television formed only a fraction of people's entertainment and the majority of people would go out in the evenings. There were still three cinemas to choose from – the Odeon, Central and Gaumont. For live entertainment, one of the four theatres could probably meet one's needs, although only two operated all year round. Knightstone Theatre reopened after the war and offered a wide variety of mainly music-hall style shows. The Playhouse had been opened in 1946 by converting the redundant Market Hall using the £3000 paid out in War Reparations for the loss of the Grove Park Pavilion. It served the town well for twenty years, until in 1964 fire broke out, destroying most of the building. Afterwards, the council discussed the possibility of building a theatre in a different area, but instead the site was enlarged by purchasing two properties in Worthy Lane and a new theatre was designed to make the most of the limited space. The new Playhouse was opened in 1969. The decorative panels on the façade are the work of a London sculptor, William Mitchell, who also did work for Liverpool Cathedral. In the summer there was also the Madeira Cove Pavilion and The Arena, a marquee with a small stage situated in Ellenborough Park, where concert parties played.

Knightstone Island
before the closure of the
buildings. On the left is
the 1832 Bath House
alongside the Swimming
Baths and Theatre.

In addition to the Open Air Pool and Knightstone swimming baths, Knightstone Medicinal Baths still offered foam, vapour, hot seawater and seaweed baths. At Weston Airport, Western Airways resumed services after their fleet was requisitioned during the war, and ran a daily service to Cardiff, summer pleasure flights and air taxis to any part of Britain. However, its pre-war promise was never fulfilled and after several years of use by gliders and light aircraft, the airport closed in the early 1980s. In 2002, the site was sold to Persimmon Homes who plan to develop it for residential, community and leisure use.

Steamer trips to and from Birnbeck Pier were restarted in 1946, but once again the fleet had been severely depleted by the war, three having been lost in the Dunkirk evacuations. Bad weather and high losses resulted in one ship being sent to the breakers and three others laid up. In 1963 a motor vessel was introduced into the fleet and a brief trial was run with hovercraft operating between Penarth and Weston. In 1965 two more motor vessels were purchased, as they were cheaper to operate, and the last paddle-steamers were scrapped. Even this move was not enough to save the trade and 1971 saw the final season of regular passenger steamer services from Birnbeck Pier. The pier, like many other enterprises, never really recovered from the war. After the steamers stopped calling its fate seemed sealed. It is currently derelict, aside from the 1902 lifeboat house which is still in use by the RNLI, and its future remains uncertain. Paddlesteamers have returned to Weston however, as the Waverley now calls each year for a summer season, having reverted to using Knightstone Harbour to embark passengers.

By the 1970s foreign resorts had taken over as the destination for most families and all British seaside resorts faced a period of decline with Weston no exception. The town faced a long and difficult battle to gain new audiences and tread new directions.

In 1974 local government reorganization resulted in the new county of Avon being formed. Weston Borough Council was abolished and the town became the seat of local government for the District of Woodspring. This area covered the northern part of Somerset from the outskirts of Bristol to Weston-super-Mare and included the towns of Nailsea, Clevedon and Portishead. The move resulted in a huge increase in staff to run the much larger authority so an extension to the town hall was built. The Albert Memorial Hall behind Emmanuel church was demolished, allowing the new building to be connected to the existing town hall. In 1995, Local Government was again the subject of review and Avon in its turn was abolished. Weston is now part of the unitary authority of North Somerset, with the same boundaries as Woodspring.

Now came the first stirrings of interest in the legacy of the Victorian builders. Changing social habits resulted in the closure of many of the old private schools and hotels. This was not a time when any virtue was seen in preserving the past and, as they became vacant, many of these buildings were demolished and replaced by anonymous blocks of flats. Etonhurst, Villa Rosa, La Retraite and Glentworth Hall were all lost in this manner. It should be said that Victorian developers were not above similar action. Swiss Villa and Coombe, Churchill and Myrtle Cottages were just a few of the older buildings lost in redevelopments between 1870 and 1910. In 1975 Weston Civic Society was formed to campaign for a more sympathetic approach to Weston's Victorian past. Today, developers are more likely to look at conversion of old buildings rather than automatic destruction. North Somerset Museum was one of the first examples of this approach. In 1975, on local government reorganization, the library and museum services were separated, the library falling under

A commemorative keyring, given to all staff, marking the end of the Borough of Weston-super-Mare, 1974.

Villa Rosa apartment block, built in 1971 on the site of the mansion of the same name in Shrubbery Road.

Avon and the museum under Woodspring District. A new home was needed for the museum and fortuitously, at the same time, the Gaslight Company workshops and stores in Burlington Street were vacated by the Gas Board. The consequent development won a Sunday Times architectural award for the quality of the conversion. Today the General Hospital, Royal Hospital and Locking Road School are just a few other examples of successful reuse of old buildings.

In 1988, following deregulation of bus services, the seafront bus station, built sixty years previously on the site of Belvedere, Weston's first private mansion, was demolished. Its loss, and continued lack of replacement, has caused much controversy as travellers have to wait for coaches on the seafront or in Locking Road car park, neither place offering much in facilities or shelter. However, the car is now king, and major road schemes have taken priority to try and ease traffic flow. The M5 was built in 1970, allowing easy access both north and south. Many traders thought that travellers would stay on the motorway and bypass Weston altogether, but the town remains an easy distance from many cities and has retained its day tripper market. Traffic congestion in the town itself however has now become the major problem. In 2002 a new traffic plan has resulted in the closure of many town centre roads to traffic other than buses, increasing the pedestrianised areas. While this may make shopping a more pleasant experience, it makes getting here harder as more cars are forced into fewer roads!

So what of the future? In the mid-1990s 'Turning the Tide', a heritage and environment strategy for a seaside resort, was published by the English Tourist Board and the Civic Trust using Weston-super-Mare as a model. The Tourism and Development Action Plan was formed as a three-year partnership between the public and private sectors with a brief to produce recommendations to regenerate Weston-super-Mare as a leading family seaside resort. One of the key areas of action was the re-appraisal of the Victorian and Edwardian heritage of Weston. The town still retains much of its original charm with streets of limestone houses, parks, the piers and of course the sands, but today's tourists are very demanding. In addition, holiday patterns have changed and people are now more likely to take several short breaks a year. Residential growth has also been rapid and these people also have their needs, such as good shops, leisure facilities and essentially, work. During the last third of the twentieth century Weston was the fastest-growing area in Europe, with huge new housing estates built at Worle and Locking Castle. Unfortunately employment has not seen the same growth and 75 per cent of residents now have to commute to Bristol and other towns, leading to traffic gridlock at peak periods. It is vital that more jobs are created locally and the recent purchase by the South West Development Agency of the redundant RAF station at Locking may offer some hope.

This clock, on the Beach Lawns near the Tourist Information Centre, is all that remains today of Weston bus station.

Certainly some initiatives have taken place in recent years to improve the surroundings and amenities and to carry the resort into the twenty-first century. These include the Sovereign Shopping Centre and the Weston Aquarium. However the future of Knightstone Island, following the closure of the baths and theatre, remains unknown. Where once such amenities were provided by public money, they must now rely on private investment and that can be hard to encourage when decline is so evident. It is likely that, to fund any restoration of the public buildings the council will have to allow residential development.

Nevertheless, people still feel drawn to the seaside. You only need to see the crowds on the beach on a sunny summer day. Weston desperately needs investment and new attractions but still has a surprising amount of quality architecture left, including a number of elegant Regency buildings, a fact that often goes unrealized. Let us hope that in the future, Weston can attract the quality of development combined with a depth of vision that it achieved in the past.

The Sovereign shopping centre, opened in 1992.

Walking Tours

Tour 1

This walk starts in Grove Park and follows what is left of Village Weston and the early seaside resort. If time and physical ability allow, then the tour can be extended to take in Worlebury Iron Age hillfort. Wheelchair users should be able to follow the main tour without much difficulty, although a flight of steps mean a detour at Claremont Crescent. Access to the hillfort also would have to be done separately via Worlebury Hill Road. The walk is circular and may be started at any point. Allow approximately two hours.

Start at the war memorials in Grove Park.

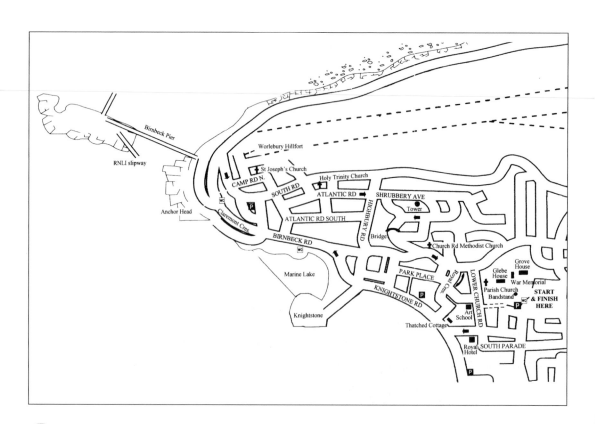

There are two memorials here. The figure of winged Victory was installed in 1922 to commemorate those killed in the First World War. Behind it is a simpler Second World War memorial. In 2001, two additional stones were placed either side to record those killed in wars and conflicts since 1945. Next to the memorial is Grove House, once the home of the lords of the manor. Most of the building was destroyed by a bomb during the Second World War but the coach house, built about 1884, remains as the right-hand part of the present building. The Smyth Pigott coat of arms can still be seen in the gable. The bungalow was built in the 1950s and houses the Mayor's Parlour.

Walk down through the park.

The bandstand was built in 1890 when the park was given to the town by Cecil Smyth-Pigott, the last lord of the manor of Weston. Bands still play here on Sundays during the summer.

Walk towards the right-hand entrance into the car park and pause in the gateway.

To your left, where the toilets now stand, was the Grove Park Pavilion. Here concert parties and pierrots would entertain visitors and residents. Like Grove House, it was destroyed by a bomb in 1942. The same bomb blew part of the iron railings into the top of the tree on the left of this entrance. You can still see them in the very top of the trunk.

These cast-iron park railings were blown up into this tree when a high explosive bomb was dropped nearby in 1941.

Grove House in Grove Park was the home of the lords of the manor of Weston. It suffered a direct hit during the air raids of 1941 and today only the coach house survives.

Walking Tour

Walk out through the car park and pause outside the entrance.

In front of you, Wadham Street Baptist church was designed by Hans Price and built in the 1860s. It is now the Blakehay, an arts venue and community centre.

Turn right to walk along Lovers' Walk and pause in the centre.

Lovers' Walk was the route taken by couples on their way to be married at the parish church. The large house next to the church is Glebe House. This was once the Rectory and parts of it date back to the sixteenth century, making it the oldest surviving building in Weston. A new rectory was built in 1889 and Glebe House is now divided up into private apartments. Up to the 1870s, it fronted a meadow, now covered by the Sensory Garden and tennis courts.

Walk to the end of Lovers' Walk and pause.

Across the road is the School of Science and Art, again one of Price and Wooler's designs. To the left of it is Weston College, opened in 1970 and substantially enlarged and altered in 1998. This was originally the site of the National School.

Cross over and turn left, walking around the College and towards the seafront. Pause on the corner.

The parish church with Glebe House, once the Rectory, on the right. Note the bare hillside at the top of Lower Church Road.

This last remaining part of Leeves' Cottage was converted into a restaurant in the 1920s.

Across the road are the stables of the Royal Hotel. This was the first purpose-built hotel in Weston, started in 1807. The original part is the square, three-storey building with veranda, facing the Sovereign Centre. The ballroom and back part were added in later years.

> **Continue towards the sea. As you get close to the seafront, on the right is the Thatched Cottage restaurant. Stop here for a moment.**

The Old Thatched Cottage Restaurant was Weston's first summer holiday home. It was built by the Revd Leeves in 1791. At that time, before the promenade was built, it was on the beach. Much of it was destroyed by a fire but a tiny part remains. On the right of the Thatched Cottage are Nos 1 and 2 Beachfield Villas. They were built by Thomas Harrill in the early 1830s on the site of what had been Sheppard's Farmhouse and a coalyard. At the time they were thought much too grand for the village; indeed the rector, Archdeacon Law, asked Harrill what on earth had possessed him to build two such big houses in Weston as he would never find anyone with enough means to live in them!

> **Continue along the path, crossing over onto the promenade at the pedestrian crossing. Turn right towards Knightstone.**

Across the road on your right, are three attractive terraces built between 1837 and 1840. They are, from the right, Victoria Buildings, Albert Buildings and Princes Buildings. Today, most have had extra storeys added

Walking Tour

Royal Crescent, after restoration of the central part in 2001.

and the gardens have been tarmacked, but there is one house still in its original state. It is the last house on the right hand side of Victoria Buildings, beside the Victoria Hall Hotel.

> **Stand and face the Park Place putting green.**

The Melrose car park and two putting greens were once a private pleasure garden for the houses surrounding them. A few of the original trees survive. On the right of the car park is Royal Crescent. It has recently undergone some restoration and looks much as it would have done when built in 1847. The row of houses facing you is Park Place, while the terrace on the left is Greenfield Place.

> **Continue along the promenade. As you reach Knightstone, turn left onto the island.**

The smaller building to the left is the Bath House built by Dr Fox in 1832. The other two buildings – a swimming baths and theatre – were both opened in 1902. The theatre, built in an Italianate style, was a popular music hall venue and many of today's well-known stars started on the repertory circuit and appeared there including Morecambe and Wise. The pool was home to Weston-super-Mare Water Polo Club with its star player, Paul Radmilovic, Olympic gold medallist. Both are closed, awaiting redevelopment.

One of the wooden seafront markers, carved by sculptor Michael Fairfax.

> **Turn around and walk back towards the promenade, carrying on northwards staying on the promenade beside the Marine Lake. If you cannot manage steps, take the route along the roadside towards Claremont as far as Birnbeck Pier.**

The Marine Lake on your left was built in 1928. Before it was enclosed by the causeway, it was a natural rocky bay called Glentworth where the ladies' bathing machines were sited. The wooden post is one of a number of seafront sculptures, carved by Michael Fairfax.

> **Carry on, bearing left around the bay. You will come to two shelters, a Victorian rotunda and a modern brick shelter.**

The Cove Pavilion once stood here. Its position is marked by a commemorative plaque in the modern shelter. Here concert parties and bands played to visitors.

Continue round the bay.

The large crescent is Claremont, completed in 1867. The sea wall on your left was part of the 1885 Sea Front Improvement Scheme, a massive engineering feat that took three years to complete.

Continue along the promenade to Anchor Head, just past the RNLI shop.

Anchor Head is a small rocky cove with a slipway for boats. It was originally the ladies' bathing place where the 'dipper', Betty Muggleworth, presided. Later, fishermen used the slipway to take visitors on trips round the bay. If you look at the rocks, you can see an outcrop of the pink limestone, used for many of the town's buildings.

Above you are two of the early hotels. The Claremont Hotel (now the Captain's Cabin) and the Royal Pier Hotel on its left, were both built in 1854. The Beatles stayed in the Royal Pier Hotel when they appeared at the Odeon cinema for a week in 1963.

Continue round the promenade and up the steps.

Anchor Head from a print of 1871. Note the lack of buildings on Birnbeck Pier. The amusements, pavilion and lifeboat house were all built from the 1890s onwards. The building on the right is the Royal Pier Hotel.

Walking Tour

Cast-iron plaque in the centre of the roadway to Birnbeck Pier.

Birnbeck Pier was built in 1867. Between 1898 and 1923 there was another jetty on the southern side of the pier so that steamers could berth at all stages of the tide. Only the northern jetty is left today. Just where the pier meets the island is the lifeboat house. This has the longest slipway of any RNLI lifeboat house in the country and is still in regular use, despite the fact that the pier itself is closed to the public as it is now unsafe. Round towards the road, the small half-timbered building was restored in 2001. It used to be a small café with a ticket office downstairs for Campbell's paddle steamers. Inside is a small display on the history of Birnbeck Pier, run by the Friends of the Old Pier.

> **Walk up the steps beside the Royal Pier Hotel, through the car park and cross over the road.**

Note the Victorian cast-iron notice set into the road notifying ownership by the Weston-super-Mare Pier Company.

> **Walk up the steps beside the public toilets and through Prince Consort Gardens out onto Kewstoke Road, or, if you cannot manage steps, turn left and continue along the road turning sharp right and back along Kewstoke Road to the gates of Prince Consort Gardens. Walk up Camp Road North opposite. If you wish to visit Worlebury Iron Age Hillfort, turn left and up the steps at the end. You will then enter the Hillfort through one of its original gateways. Continue the walk by exiting down the same steps and back into Camp Road. If you do not wish to visit the hillfort, continue straight on.**

St Joseph's church on your left was built in 1858. It was the first Roman Catholic church in Weston.

> **Turn right and then left into South Road and pause when you get to the corner of Trinity Road.**

South Road was built between 1850 and 1870. These buildings were for the wealthier residents of the town. The houses have spectacular views and large gardens. Most also had separate stable blocks and large staff quarters. Today they are too big for one family and have been converted into flats.

Cross over and walk down beside Holy Trinity Church and then left into Atlantic Road, continuing along Atlantic Road towards Highbury Road.

Walking Tour

These two terraces with the central church were built in the 1860s. The congregation was wealthy and the church was derogatively known as the 'bonnet shop' in the nineteenth century when this area of the town was known as Cliftonville. The large building on the left corner of Highbury Road was St Faith's, one of Weston's many private schools. The school bellcote can still be seen on the roof.

Cross over into Shrubbery Avenue.

When the Shrubbery was a private estate a lodge stood on the left-hand side, where the modern chalet bungalow now is, and there was a gate across the road. You could only enter on paying a fee.

Carry straight on along Shrubbery Avenue and stop by the Water Tower on your right.

The Shrubbery Water Tower, from a panoramic print of the 1860s.

Walking Tour

This was built by Sophia Rooke, over the site of a well. It housed pumping machinery and supplied all the houses on the Shrubbery Estate with fresh water until a mains supply was piped in in the 1870s. Note the carved heads of wild animals around the top. It is now a private residence.

> **Walk down Tower Walk and turn right at the end. Walk along Shrubbery Road, past Shrubbery Walk, turn left at the end and down under the little bridge.**

This private bridge linked the two parts of the garden of Villa Rosa, the mansion built for Sophia Rooke in 1844. The house was demolished in 1969 and the two large blocks of flats built, although the coach house survives as a private residence now called Villa Rosetta.

> **Carry straight on and at the end of the road turn left into Upper Church Road.**

The lodge on the right corner was one of three guarding the entrance to the Shrubbery Estate. It has a date stone over the front door of 1839. The Methodist church on the left was designed by Hans Price and built in 1881. It is surprisingly ornate for a Methodist chapel.

> **Walk along the road, keeping to the left-hand side. You will come to Victoria Park on the left.**

On the right is another, better, view of Royal Crescent. In the road close to the wall post-box is an example of one of the drain covers cast at the foundry of W. Hillman in Richmond Street. It bears the mark of Joseph Coles, Contractor, Clevedon.

> **Continue along the road, turning right at the junction, and walk down Lower Church Road.**

On the left is the parish church of St John the Baptist. The churchyard contains the graves of many Weston villagers. There is also a fine yew tree on the northern side. If you walk round to the east end you can see the old rectory and its stables. On the north side of the covered passageway is the original gateway used by the rector to reach the church. The church is open most mornings if you wish to see inside. There are some fine marble memorials in the chancel, including one to Colonel Rogers who died after trying to save the two Elton boys from drowning in 1819.

Return to Lower Church Road.

On your right is Oriel Terrace, built in 1847 in the Elizabethan style. Note the fine carved name panel in the centre of the terrace.

Turn left along Lover's Walk and back into Grove Park. If you wish to complete your walk on a modern note, visit the garden built in memory of Jill Dando. It is situated just in front of Grove House.

Jill Dando was a BBC presenter, well-known for shows such as *Holiday*. Jill grew up in Weston and spent her early working life on the local newspaper. She was murdered on the doorstep of her London home in April 1999 and is buried at Ebdon Road cemetery. In July 2001 this garden was laid out in her memory. It was designed by Alan Titchmarsh and constructed by the *Ground Force* television team in just three days.

This walk has taken you along the routes used by Weston's villagers and early visitors. Whilst the roads are now surfaced and lined with buildings, they follow the tracks to the common fields on the hillside and the early bathing places, up to the settlement used by our ancestors in the Iron Age and across the creek that flowed to Grove Park. I hope you were able to picture these places as they once were.

Headstone of the Hancock family, in the graveyard of the parish church.

Tour 2

This walk illustrates the contrast between the Victorian mansions, the Edwardian semi-detached villas and the small working-class terraces in the town centre. Whilst taking public footpaths and main streets, it does mean a reasonably steep walk up Montpelier. However, the walk is circular and may be started at any point. Allow approximately one and a half hours.

> **Start at the Museum in Burlington Street and turn right. At the end of the road cross over and turn left into Alfred Street, walking towards the Boulevard.**

On the corner of Prospect Place is the old Christ Church Parish Hall, now a scooter museum. Although the church is in Montpelier, the parish of Christ Church reaches down as far as Baker Street. Opposite the Parish Hall is the original hospital, designed by Hans Price. You can see a datestone of 1865 in the gable, although the hospital did not actually open until October 1866.

> *Cross over Hans Price Crescent, a new road built when the hospital buildings were converted into private housing in the 1990s, and turn right into the Boulevard at the traffic lights.*

The building on your right was originally Weston General Hospital. In the 1920s, a fund-raising drive, led by local entrepreneur Henry Butt, raised £50,000, sufficient for a large new hospital furnished with all the latest equipment. It was opened in July 1928 by the Duke and Duchess of York, later King George VI and Queen Elizabeth. With various additions and alterations over the years, it served the people of Weston until 1986, when the present hospital was built at Uphill.

The building next to the hospital is the Library and Museum. Prior to this building opening, the museum was housed in the Albert Memorial Hall behind Emmanuel church in Oxford Street while the public library was in Grove House in Grove Park. The money was raised to mark Queen Victoria's Diamond Jubilee and the foundation stone was laid in 1899. It is one of the few buildings in the town built of red brick. Designed in the Art Nouveau style, the carvings of the muses are by Harry Hems. In 1975, the library and museum services separated and the museum collections were moved to Burlington Street. Next to the library is the telephone exchange which opened in 1969.

> *Carry on along the road.*

Look out for interesting architectural details on the houses as you pass. For example, Nos 2 and 4 Gerard Road have the heads of medieval kings carved over their ground-floor windows.

> *Cross over at the pedestrian crossing, turn left and then sharp right up Christchurch Path North into Montpelier. If you cannot manage steps, turn right after crossing over and then first left up Montpelier.*

North Somerset Museum in Burlington Street. This was built in 1912 as the Gaslight Company workshops and stores. It was converted for use as a museum in 1975.

Walking Tour

Christ Church during the building of the new chancel in 1878.

Montpelier was one of Weston's private estates with a lodge at the northern entrance, still there today. The older houses on the left were built in the late 1850s and once looked out onto parkland. This was then built on in the 1930s which is why the houses on the right are more modern. Christ Church was built in 1855 on land donated to the town by local developer Henry Davies. Architect Hans Price was a regular worshipper here, and designed the new chancel, added in 1878.

Walk up Montpelier, turning right into Trewartha Park keeping to the left and bearing left at the junctions.

These villas are mostly 1890s in date and you can see the influence of the Art Nouveau style in their design. Note the date stone of 1898 on the gable of No. 9.

Stop outside No. 7.

This house, originally called Bourn, was designed by Hans Price as his personal residence. Turn right round to face west and you can glimpse a large house behind high walls, between the modern houses. This is Trewartha, once the home of Henry Pethick, whose daughter, Emmeline, was a leading light in the suffragette cause. In 1906 she was co-founder, with the Pankhursts, of the London Committee of the Women's Social and Political Union. Together with her husband Fred Lawrence, publisher of the magazine *Votes for Women*, they were arrested on several occasions with

Decorative stonework over a doorway of a house in Trewartha Park.

Emmeline suffering the horrors of being force fed in Holloway Prison.

At the top of the road turn right and walk along Bristol Road. Turn right and enter Weston Cemetery.

The Lodge at the entrance is built of the attractive pink limestone, quarried on site. A vein of this stone runs through the hillside and outcrops at Anchor Head. Facing you is a mortuary chapel. This was once one of a pair, the surviving one for members of the Church of England, while the other, now demolished, was for Nonconformists. Just behind the chapel is a memorial to Belgian refugees who fled to Weston during the First World War.

Walk down through the cemetery.

On the ridge, close to the War Memorial, there are no graves. This is because the ground is broken by caves or old underground mine shafts. Weston and the surrounding villages once had a thriving mining industry and shafts and galleries made in search of lead, zinc and iron ores lie under Weston Woods, Worlebury Golf Course and even some streets! Near the bottom is a group of Commonwealth war graves, together with those of civilians who were killed in Weston during the Second World War.

As you leave the cemetery, pause by the gate.

The lodge and gate at this southern entrance were originally those for Ashcombe House before The Drive was built. Ashcombe House was a large mansion built for the Capell family in the 1830s. The lodge was built later.

Cross over at the traffic lights and walk down Ashcombe Road.

The chemist's shop on the corner was once the stationmaster's house for the Weston, Clevedon & Portishead Light Railway. The main Weston station for this line was just down the lane on the left of the shop. Opened in 1897, it was the only direct link between the three seaside towns, closing in 1940.

Ashcombe Road follows the line of one of the old drove ways. The house on the south west corner of Ashcombe Road and Clarendon Road

W.C & P.L.RLY

NOTICE.

PASSENGERS ARE REQUESTED TO EXAMINE THEIR TICKETS & CHANGE BEFORE LEAVING THE BOOKING OFFICE. AS NO MISTAKES AFTERWARDS CAN BE RECOGNISED.

By Order.

Enamel sign from the Weston, Clevedon and Portishead Light Railway. (Collections of North Somerset Museum Service)

is St Duthus. This was once the home of Conway Warne, owner of the Royal Potteries from 1885 until his death in 1923. Further down the road is The Ashcombe pub. This building is older than most of the others in the street and catered for the workers at the Potteries, which were in the middle of what were then open fields to your left.

> **At the end of Ashcombe Road pause and look left.**

Across the road is St Saviour's church. This is now closed and will probably be demolished as it is unsafe. It was built in 1892 to serve the new housing estates then being built in this area.

> **Turn right into Locking Road staying on the northern side of the road.**

There is a wide variety of building styles here. Note the older houses with plain symmetrical façades, dotted amongst the later Victorian properties with architectural details such as terracotta tiles decorating the window

bays. On the corner of Locking Road and Swiss Road is an antiquarian bookshop and other small shops. The whole of this corner, right back to Beaufort Road, was once the site of Swiss Villa and its gardens. This gothic-style villa was the home of solicitor, Joseph Edgar. It was here that Brunel is reputed to have stayed whilst the Bristol & Exeter Railway was being constructed. Only the lodge survives today, on the west corner of Swiss and Locking Roads.

> **Carry on along Locking Road. George Street is the second road on your right.**

If you wish you can walk halfway up George Street, to look at the small terraced villa on the western side where Lord Alexander was born. Albert Alexander was born at 33 George Street in 1883. He became a politician and later First Lord of the Admiralty during the Second World War. Look for the blue plaque. If you look at the buildings in George Street from Locking Road, you can see that the houses at this end of the street are different in style from those further along. This is because this end of the street is older, being built in 1853. The road was then a cul-de-sac like Little George Street and Camden Terrace. This area was known as 'Camden Town' and housed many of the workers at the Royal Potteries.

> **Return to Locking Road and continue towards the sea.**

On the left-hand side of the road, where Tesco and its car park are now, were the railway goods yards and cattle market. Next to the goods station were the excursion platforms. Hundreds of passengers would pour out of this station and make their way along Regent Street to the beach.

> **Walk along Alexandra Parade.**

You will pass a small half-timbered building in the centre. This was once a weighbridge. Alma Street, on your right, was named after the battle of the Alma River in September 1854, during the Crimean War.

> **Cross to the centre at the pedestrian crossing just past Orchard Street and turn left to walk into the centre of the gardens.**

Walking Tour

This area was the site of the first station, built in 1841. A level crossing took the track across Locking Road at what is now the entrance to Tesco, and then along these gardens into the station, now the site of the Floral Clock. The pub, currently called Jack Stamp's, was then called the Railway Hotel and was separated from the station by a narrow footpath. The Art Deco-style Odeon Cinema of 1935 is now a listed building. On the other side of Walliscote Road is an impressive terrace called Magdala Buildings. This was designed by Price and Wooler.

> **Turn right and walk towards the Floral Clock.**

The clock was built in 1935, with a cuckoo added in 1951 to mark the Festival of Britain. It became one of Weston's most well-known landmarks and crowds would gather to watch the cuckoo appear.

> **Walk round the Floral Clock and cross back over the pedestrian crossing and turn left down Orchard Street.**

Meadow Street and Orchard Street were once part of the farm belonging to Farmer King, where Charlotte Wilson and her mother stayed in 1826. In the 1850s the area was developed with small shops. There are still a few original shop fronts left today.

> **Carry on over the traffic lights, taking the next right into Burlington Street and the Museum.**

This is the end of the tour. I hope you have enjoyed this walk illustrating the wide variety of domestic architecture lining Weston's streets. You could now visit the museum. Inside are archaeological finds and other displays on Weston's past.

The Next Steps

If you would like to find out more about Weston-super-Mare there are a variety of sources available.

Weston Library in the Boulevard has a large Local Studies Collection, including directories, census returns and guide books. Copies of the local newspapers are held on microfilm, and there are collections of maps, ephemera and photographs.

North Somerset Museum Service in Burlington Street also has a large local history collection, including original photographs, documents, paintings and over 3000 postcards of Weston. Their files may be consulted by appointment.

The Heritage Centre in Wadham Street has displays on the fabric of the town.

The Somerset County Record Office is the main repository for original deeds, leases, indentures, maps and other material relating to the history of Somerset and Weston-super-Mare, which may be viewed by appointment.

There have been a number of books written about Weston-super-Mare in recent years and the following are just a few recommendations:

Beisley, P., *Weston-super-Mare Past* (2001)
Brown, B. & Loosley, J., The *Book of Weston* (1979)
Brown, B. & Loosley, J., *Yesterday's Town – Weston-super-Mare* (1985)
Knight, F. A., *The Seaboard of Mendip* (1902, reprinted 1988)
Moore, G.M., *The Good Earth – A study of market gardening in Worle and Milton* (1999)
Poole, S. P., *Weston-super-Mare in Old Photographs* (1987)
Poole, S. P., *Weston-super-Mare in Old Photographs – the 1950s* (1991)
Poole, S. P., *Weston-super-Mare, Archive Photographs Series* (1997)
Poole, S. P., *Weston-super-Mare in Old Photographs – 1950s–1970s* (2001)
Poole, S. P., *Weston-super-Mare, A Pictorial History* (1995)
Terrell, S., *Birnbeck Pier – A Short History* (1996, revised 2001)

Index